RAINBOW SONGS

Ananda's Spiritual Songbook

Ananda Jaroslaw Istok

ISBN: 978-0-244-74335-2

Preface for the first Edition

Who has already leafed through songbooks where most of the songs are unknown? Not with this book! Because all songs are linked to video or audio files, and indeed smart, because even if Youtube deletes the video, the link target is changed, although of course the printed version remains constant. Please report any overlooked dead links at ananda@rainbowsongs.org.

The book is for the Rainbow Family and all spiritually interested people who like to sing in the groups. It is new in form, compact and modern. Each song includes a QR code to the video or audio file. The short links come with it. The video thumbnail allows for quick recognition.

Because of the compactness, the Letter sizes are flexible. Musical signs of the repetition (from//: to: //) and mostly European chords spelling Am = a are used. Chord changing ware *italianized* in text. There will surely be more songs over time. At the beginning almost 300 songs come together on about 100 pages. Buyers always have guaranteed access to the ever-current online edition. Anyone can also submit songs anonymously, keeping a community alive.

Thanks for the support also by the purchase

Om Namaha Shivaya, Namaste!

Ananda

Vorwort zu der ersten Ausgabe

Wer hat schon in Liederbüchern geblättert, wo die meisten Songs einem nicht bekannt sind? Nicht mit diesem Buch! Denn Alle Lieder sind mit Video oder Audio Dateien verlinkt und zwar intelligent, da selbst wenn Youtube das Video löscht, wird das Link Ziel geändert obwohl natürlich die gedruckte Version konstant bleibt. Bitte übersehene tote Links unter ananda@rainbowsongs.org hierfür melden.

Das Buch ist für die Rainbow Family und Alle spirituell interessierten Menschen, die gerne in den Gruppen singen. Es ist neu in der Form, kompakt und modern. Jedes Lied erhält einen QR Code zu der Video oder Audio Datei. Die Shortlinks kommen mit dazu. Das Video Thumbnail ermöglicht eine schnelle Erkennung.

Wegen der Kompaktheit sind die Schiftgrössen flexibel. Musikalische Zeichen der Wiederholung (von //: bis ://) und meist europäische Akkorde Schreibweise Am=a werden eingesetzt. Akkordwechsel wurde *kursiv* dargestellt. Es werden sicher mehr Lieder mit der Zeit kommen. Zu Anfang kommen da schon fast 300 Lieder auf etwa 100 Seiten zusammmen. Käufer haben immer garantierten Zugang zu der stets aktuallen Online Ausgabe. Jeder kann auch anonym Lieder einsenden und somit eine Community lebendig halten.

Danke für die Unterstützung auch durch den Kauf dieses Buches ;o)

Om Namaha Shivaya, Namaste!

Ananda

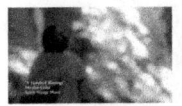

A Hundred Blessings

When *Love,*comes *suddenly* and *taps*(a, C a) *On* your *window,*run and let it *in,*but first(C a, C F)
Shut the door of your *reason* (a C) Even the smallest *hint*, *chases* love away (a, F)
Like *smoke* that *drowns*, the freshness *of* (C a, G) The morning *breeze* (F)
To *reason*, Love can only *say* (a, C) This way is *barred, you* can't pass *through* (a, C F)
But to the lover, it offers a hundred blessings (F, C a)
Before the mind *decides*, to take a *step* (C, F)
//: *Love* has *reached*, the seventh *heaven* (C a, G) Love has climbed the *Holy* Mountain :// (F)
I must stop this *talk* now, and let Love *speak* (C a, C) From its nest of silence (F)
Mirabai Ceiba: / istok.de/7499

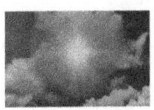

Aad Guray Nameh

Aad Guray Nameh, Jugaad Guray Nameh (C F C)(C F C)
Sat Guray Nameh,Siri Guroo *Dayvay Nameh*(C F C)(C G C)
Snatam Kaur: / istok.de/7100-1

Amrit Kirtan: / H a H a / H a H a / e H C H / e H C H / istok.de/7100-2

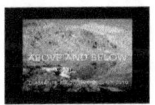

Above and Below

//: *Above* And Below And *All* Around You Are :// / a G
You Are The Essence Of All The *Beauty* Of Life / d a
You Are The Essence Of All The *Love* Of My Life / d a
//: Sacred *One* Source *Within* And *Beyond* :// / F G a
Solcircle: / istok.de/6331

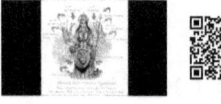 **Adi Shakti Namo Namo**

Adi Shakti, Adi Shakti / d
Adi Shakti, Namo *Namo* / C - E7
Sarab Shakti, Sarab Shakti / d
Sarab Shakti, Namo *Namo* / C - E7
Prithum Bhagvati, Prithum Bhagvati / d
Prithum Bhagvati, Namo *Namo* / C - E7
Kundalini Mata Shakti, Kundalini Mata Shakti / d
Kundalini Mata Shakti, Namo *Namo* / C - E7
Gurudass (Echo): / istok.de/6343-1

Snatam Kaur: a G a G a G... / istok.de/6343-2

Ajeet Kaur: e a e a e a... / istok.de/6343-3

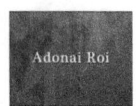 **Adonai ro-i lo ehsar**

Adonai ro-i, *Adonai ro-i* (a, C E)
//: Lo ehsar Lo *ehsar*, *Adonai ro-i* :// (F C, E a)
//: Lord *you're* my *Shepherd*, *You're* watching over *me* (a, C E)
You will meet *all* my needs, *I* wan't lack for *anything* (F C, E a)
I will trust *in* your care, *O* Shepherd of my *soul* :// (F C, E a)
Moim *pasterzem* Pan, jego *laska trwa* (a, C E)
//:Wszystko *mam* wszystko *mam*, Moim *pasterzem Pan* :// (F C, E a)
Liberated Wailing Wall: a, C E / F C, E a / istok.de/6512-1

6

Ananda (1/3):(Psalm 23):(Canon): a, C E / F C, E a / istok.de/6512-2

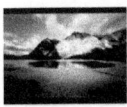

Adoramus Te Domine

Ooo - Adoramus Te Domine (GDe, a D G)
Also: Adoramus *Te* o *Christe* / *We* Adore You *Lord* Jesus
Christ
Taize: GDe, a D G / istok.de/5517

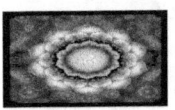

Ajai Alai

Ajai Alai Abhai abai, Abhu Aju Anais akaas
Aganj abhanj Alakh abhakh, Akaal Deyal Alekh abhekh
Anaam akaam agaah adhaah, Anaathe parmaathe Ajoni Amoni
Na Raage, na Raange, na Rupe , na Rekhe
Akarmang abharmang aganje alekhe
Invencible, indestructible , Intocable, indivisible
Sin deseo, sin miedo , Sin nacimiento, sin fin
Mas alla del amor , Mas alla del color
Mas alla de la vida, compasivo , Mas alla del amor
Mas alla del color , Mas alla de la vida, compasivo
Mirabai Ceiba (Quasi canon): a d a , d e a / istok.de/6565-1

Shri Guru Gobind Singh ji (1/3) Dilpreet Bhatia: a G a G a ... / istok.de/6565-2

7

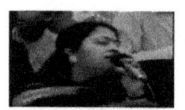

Alakh Niranjan

//: Alakh Niranjana *Bhava* Bhaya *Bhanjana* :// (a G a)
//: Narayan Nara-yan, Narayan Prabhu Narayan :// (a G a, G e a)
Didi Nisha Manikantan: a G a / a G a, G e a / <u>istok.de/6385</u>

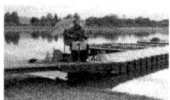

All I ask of You

//: All I ask of *You* is forever to *remember* Me as loving *you* :// (G e C G)
//: I sch-k Allah Mabut-L'ila, I sch-k *Allah Mabut-L'ila* :// (G C D G, C D G)
Paul Fresh: (G e C G)(G C D G, C D G) / <u>istok.de/5307</u>

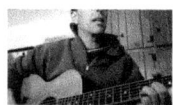

All will be well

All will be *well,* And *all* will be *well* / a d, G e
All *manner* of *things* will be *well* / F G d
Act on Wisdom: / <u>istok.de/6241</u>

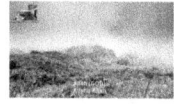

Allah Hu

//: Allah Hu Allah Hu, Allah Hu Allah :// (x4) (a G, F E)
//: As I look to natures beauty ...dazzled am I (a G, F E)
knowing Everything calls on you, The Lord most high ://(a G, F E)
Labbayk, Sami Yousuf & Coskun): a G F E / <u>istok.de/5812</u>

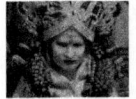

Amba Bhavani Jaya Jagadamba

//: *Amba* Bhavani, *Jaya* Jaga*damba* :// (C, G C)
Natascia Tara: / istok.de/6351

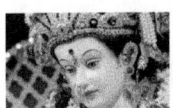

Amba Taye

Amba Amba taye, Akilandeshwari nije, Anapurneshwari taye (a)
Oooo *Adi* para Shakti *nije* (E a)
Yashoda Emam: / istok.de/5338-1

Omkara: / istok.de/5338-2

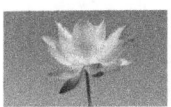

Amma Take me away

Take me away won't you *carry* me, *Let* me rest in your *arms* for a *while* (a G, F G a)
Take me away won't you *carry* me, *Let* me bath in the *sweetness* of your *smile*
Amma *take me away*, Won't you *take me away* (C G a, C G a)
Songs of the Heart: a G F G a / C G a / istok.de/5417

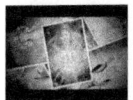

Ananda Rupam Hairakkhand

Anandarupam citi *shakti diptam*, *Vidyam* param *brahmarasanubhutim* (C dG, C dGC)
Karunya purnam guru *murti rupam*, *Devim* namamah *jagadi-shvarin tvam* (C dG, C dGC)
Mam *raksa* nityam *jagadavalambe*, *Tvameva* satyam *jagaj-jivani mata* (C dG, C dGC)
Sansara janma *jvarroga-vaidya*, *Madyam* bhaje *haidakhandavasinim* (C dG, C dGC)
Sara svati: C dG, C dGC (melody from Twameva Mata): istok.de/5476

9

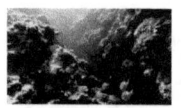

Ancient Mother

Ancient *Mother* I hear Your *calling*, Ancient *Mother* I hear Your *song* (G a, C G a)
Ancient *Mother* I hear Your *calling*, Ancient *Mother* I hear Your *song* (G a, F G a)
CHOIR: Ishtar, Cerredwin, Hecate, Inanna Isis, Artemis, Sophia, Athena
Coatilicue, Aphrodite, Mielikki, Astarte Gaia, Saraswati, Kali // Pele, Paso Wee,
Demeter, ParvatiHera, Akewa, Diana, Nidaba Chicomecoatl, Lilith,
Shekhina, Morgana Maya, Izanami, Shakti
Robert Gass: Ga,CGa , Ga,FGa / istok.de/5481

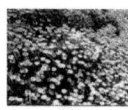

Ancient Mother by Sacred Earth

Ancient *Mother* I hear you *calling* me, Ancient *Mother* I hear your *song* / C G, a E
Ancient *Mother* I hear your *laughter*, Ancient *Mother* I taste your *tears* / C G, a E
//: *Shuna* ama yo yo, hey hey :// 4x / C, G, a, E
//: You are the *water* that I drink, you are the *air* that I breath / C G
You are the *sun* who gives me warm, you are the *earth* beneath my fit :// a E
...Ancient...Shuna...
//: Open your *heart* open your *mind*, feel your *Soul* fly your *dream* :// C G, a E
Sacred Earth: C G, a E / istok.de/7359

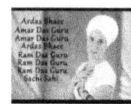

Ardas Bhaee

Ardas Bahee, Amar Das Guru Amar *Das* Guru, Ardas Bahee A E
Ram Das Guru, *Ram* Das Guru *Ram* Das Guru, *Sachee* Sahee h D6 E A
Ardas Bahee, Amar *Das* Guru, Amar *Das* Guru, *Ardas* Bahee A D A E
Ram Das Guru, *Ram* Das Guru, *Ram* Das Guru, *Sachee* Sahee h E D6 A
Nirinjan Kaur: / istok.de/5734

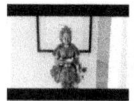

Asato Ma Sad Gamaya

OM ASATO MA SAD GAMAYA (a)

10

TAMASO MA JYOTIR *GAMAYA* (E)
MRITYOR MA *AMRITAM* GAMAYA (a)
OM *SHANTI* SHANTI SHANTI (a)
Deva Premal & Miten: a E a / <u>istok.de/6747-1</u>

Shiva Mantra Version(acapella ot 1 tone)/ <u>istok.de/6747-2</u>

Sai Baba: a E a, a E a, d a, E a / <u>istok.de/6747-3</u>

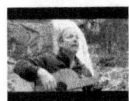

Auch eine Reise von Tausend Meilen

Auch eine *Reise* von *Tausend* Mailen, *Fängt* mit dem *ersten Schritt* an /a G A, a G a
Vertraue und *gehe*, *Vertraue* und *gehe* / C G, C G
Wolfgang Bossinger & Katharina Neubronner: / <u>istok.de/5855</u>

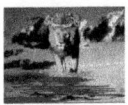

Baruch Hashem Ha Mashiah Yeshua

//: *Baruch Hashem* Ha *Mashiah Yeshua, Baruch
Hashem Adonai* ://
Dzidek: a E a E, a E a -E / <u>istok.de/6322</u>

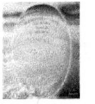

Be one says the Lord

Be *one* says the Lord Be one says the Lord Be one be one with me (d)
Love all *serve* all, Be *one* be one with *me* (C d, A7 d)
Ananda: d, C d A7 d / <u>istok.de/5447</u>

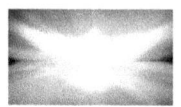 # Be Still

[*Be* still and *know* that I am (a e) Be still and *know* (a)]
[*Be* still, *Be* still (a d) *Be* still and *know* (e a)]
Terry Oldfield & Mike Oldfield: / istok.de/7421

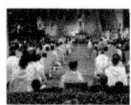 # Behüte mich Gott

Be*hüte* mich *Gott* (G (D)-e) Ich *vertraue* dir (a) Du *zeigst* mir den *Weg*(h a)
zum *Leben* ((C)G) Bei *dir* ist *Freude* ((D)e) *Freude* in *Fülle* (C (G)D)
Taize: / istok.de/7555

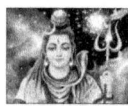 ### Bolo Bolo Sab Mil Bolo Om Namah Shivaya

[//: *Bolo* Bolo Sab Mil Bolo, *OM* Namah *Shivaya* :// (a Ea)
//: *OM* Namah *Shivaya*, *OM* Namah *Shivaya* ://] x2 (a d E a)
//: Jutha Jata Me, Ganga Dhari :// (a, E a)
//: Trishula Dhari, Damaru Bajave :// (a d, E a)
//: Dama Dama Dama-Dama, Damaru Baje :// ((a, Ea))
//: Gunj Utha OM Namah Shivaya :// (a d, E a)
OM Namah Shivaya, OM Namah Shivaya (a, d)
Hara OM Namah Shivaya (E a)
Vikram Hazra (Groovy): a Ea, a d E a / istok.de/5505

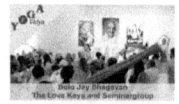 # Bolo Jay Bhagavan

//: *Everything* is *love* (ea) *Everything* is *love* (DG) :// (-E)

//: *Bolo* Jay Bhaga*van* (Ga) *Bolo* Jay Bhaga*van* (De) ://
//: God is the *source*, And the essence of it *all* (ea)
God is every*where*, God is every*where* :// (De...)
The Love Keys (Groovy, Echo) also just: G a D G: / <u>istok.de/8131-1</u>

The Love Keys in Concert (Groovy, Echo): / <u>istok.de/8131-2</u>

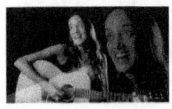

Butterfly People

On the shores of a *mystical ocean*, There lies a *cave* with a magical *door (a d a, d E a)*
All are welcome but *those* who *enter*, Never shall *return* not a *single* day *more*
Do you feel the *rhythm* of my *heart* beat, Beating in *time* with the *drum* in your *hands*
Fly away on the *waves* of the *ocean*, Seeking and *finding* the *butterfly people*
...//: *Gate* Gate *Para Gate*, Parasam-*Gate Bodhi Soha* :// (a d a, d E a)
Lindsey Wise: a d a, d E a / <u>istok.de/5508</u>

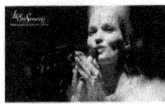

Calma E Tranquilidade

Calma e tranquilidade sao as ordens do Senhor / a
Calma e *tranquilidade* para *receber* o *Amor* - *Mmm Mmm* /d E a-ea ea
Lex van Someren, Stephanie Maria Martens: / <u>istok.de/5862-1</u>

Deva Premal: / <u>istok.de/5862-2</u>

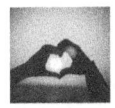

Celebrate the Light of the Sun

1)*Celebrate* the *light* of the *sun*, Show the way Lucina / a G a, a G a-G

13

Dance the round on *solstice night*, *Blessed* be the Great *Mother* / a D a, G a
2)*Celebrate* the *light* of the *moon*, *Show* the *way Lucina* / a G a, a G a-G
Dance the round on the *full* moon *night*,*Blessed* be the Great *Mother* / a D a,G a
As Canon: / istok.de/6556

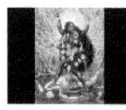

Chamundaye Kali Ma

//: *Chamundaye* Kali *Ma*, *Annapurna* Devi *Ma* :// (C F, CG C)
Kali Durge Kali Ma,*Kali Durge Kali Ma* (F C F C)
Maha Kali Kali Ma, Maha Kali Kali Ma (F C G C)
Ray Orr (Groovy): C F, CG C / F C F C, F C G C / istok.de/6642

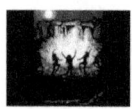

Circle Within A Circle

We are a *circle*, Within a *circle*, With no *beginning* *(e, e, D)*
And never *ending* (e)
Written by Ric Hamouris: (Em/Em/D/Em): / istok.de/6359

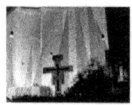

Crucem Tuam

Crucem tuam adoramus Domine,*Resurrectionem tuam laudamus Domine*/aFEa, FCEa
Laudamus et *glorificamus*, *Resurrectionem tuam laudamus Domine* / FE FE, F C E a
Taize: / istok.de/7106

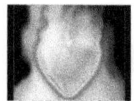

Deeper

//: *Deeper*, Deeper to The *Heart* Of *Love*, Deeper ://a F a

Letting *Go to* The *Mystery* / a G eF
Letting *Go to* The *Mystery* / a G eF
Letting *Go to* The *Mystery* a G eF
Rising, *Rising* In Love / aG , ea
Deva Premal: Intro: a e a e... / <u>istok.de/6468</u>

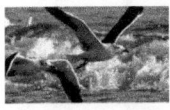

Dhanyavad Ananda

//: *Dhanyavad* Dhanyavad *Dhanyavad Ananda* (C F C)
Dhanyavad Dhanyavad Dhanyavad *Ananda* :// (a G C)
Henry Marshall: C F C, a G C / <u>istok.de/5526</u>

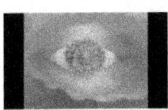

Dhanyavad Sananda

/:*Om* Namo Bhagavate *Sanandaya,Dhanyavad Sananda*:/(C a, d G)
/:*Om* Namo Bhagavate *Sanandaya*, *Dhanyavad Sananda*:/(C d, e a)
Nama Ra: C a d G, C d e a / <u>istok.de/5529</u>

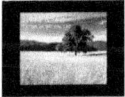

Domine dona nobis pacem

Domine, *Domine*, *dona* nobis *pacem* (a, Ea, F E)
Domine, *Domine*, *dona* nobis *pacem* (a, Ea, F G a)
Taize: a, Ea, F E / a, Ea, F G a / <u>istok.de/5523</u>

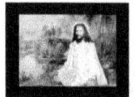

Door Of My Heart

//: *Door* of my heart. *Open* wide i give for *Thee* :// (e,C,D)
// *Will't* Thou come, will't Thou come. *Just* for once *come* to me :// (e,C,D)
//: *Will* my days fly away. *Without* seeing Thee my *Lord* :// (e,C,D)
//: *Night* by day, night by day. *I* look for Thee *night* by day :// (e,C,D)
Contribute to Paramahansa Yoganda: e,C,D / <u>istok.de/6123</u>

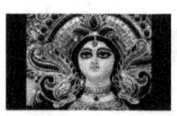

Durge Durge Durge Jai Jai Ma

Karuna Sagari *Ma*, *Kali* Kapalini *Ma* (e D, e D)
Jaga Udharini *Ma*, *Jaga* Udharini *Ma* (e D, e D)
Jagadambe Jai Jai *Ma*, *Jagadambe Jai* Jai *Ma* (C D e, C D e)
//: *Durge Durge*, *Durge Jai* Jai *Ma* :// x times...(e D , C D e)
Emam & Friends (Echo): e D , C D e / <u>istok.de/6449-1</u>

Sai Baba (Groovy with Echo): / <u>istok.de/6449-2</u>

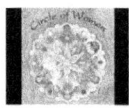

Earth My Body

//: *Earth* my *body*, *Water* my *blood* (d C, d a)
Air my *breath*, And *fire* my *spirit* :// (d C, d a)
Alice Di Micele (Echo): d C, d a / <u>istok.de/5552-1</u>

Sarva Antah (Groovy): / <u>istok.de/5552-2</u>

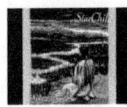

Earthchild Starchild

//: Earthchild Starchild, Now Is The Time To Open Your Hearts ://a, G a
With Our Feets, Standing On Grandmother Earth / G, a
With Our Arms, Reaching For Grandfather Sky / G, a ..//...Earthchild...
Gila Antara: / istok.de/6456

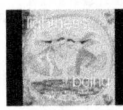

Ek Ong Kar Satguru Prasad

//: Ek Ong Kar *Satgur* Prasad , *Satguru* Prasad *Ek* Ong Kar *://* (C G)(a F)
//: Ek Ong Kar Satgur Prasad, *Satguru* Prasad *Ek* Ong Kar *://* (G)(a F)
Satkirin Kaur Khalsa: Groovy (Lightness of Being): istok.de/6463

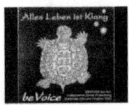

Erde Meine Mutter

//: Erde Meine Mutter, Himmel Mein Vater ://
//: Feuer Erde Wasser und Luft, Ich bin ://
BeVoice: a / acapella / istok.de/5857

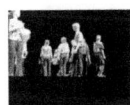

Every Part of the Eart

Every part of the *Earth*, Is sacred to my *people*
We are part of the *Earth*, And *she* is part of *us*
This we know that the *Earth*, Does *not* belong to *us* (-We belong to the Earth)
//: Our god is the *same* god *://* , *//: All beings* share the *same breath ://*
If the *beasts* were gone *we would* die, *Of* a *great* loneliness of *spirit*
//: All things are *connected ://*
Robert-Schuman-Gymnasium with drums: a G(e) a: istok.de/6578-1

As Canon acapela: / istok.de/6578-2

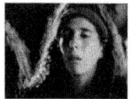

Find Yourself in Harmony

//: *Find* Yourself in *Harmony Let* Go of All Your *Fears* / G D, e C
Then *You'll* Find the *Place* to Be is Right *Here* :// / G, D -C
1)*With* the blue skies *above, What* you got to *worry* about / G D, e C
Place trust *in* your love, *Blue* skies above / G, D -C ...Find Yourself...
2)*We* all know that *life* doesn't change, *Goes* about its *own* way / G D, e C
Don't try to figure it out, *Just* see how you can play / G, D -C
3)//: *Open* up your *hearts* and sing, *Open* up your *eyes* and see / G D, e C)
All the beauty in *everything*,Is *what* you are ://G,D-C(A *Shining Star*)(GD-C)x2
Rainbow Spirit Oregon (Groovy): / istok.de/6646

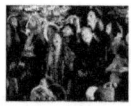

Fly Like an Eagle

//: *He* Wichi tay tay (echo), *Wichi* tay *yo* (echo) :// a, G a
Fly Like An Eagle (echo), *Flying* So *High* (echo) / a, G a
Circling The Universe (echo), On *Wings* Of Pure *Light* (echo) /a, G a
Mar7Art (Echo): / istok.de/7220

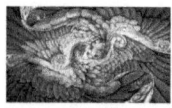

Fly like the Wind

1) //: *Fly* like the wind *run* like the water, *Moving* o'er the land for *eternity* /a e / G a
Fly like the wind *run* like the water, *Flowing* o'er the land for *eternity* ://a e / G a
2)Once we are *young* and full of *being*, Once we are *babies* and full of *seeing* /a e / G a
Once we are *strong* and full of *doing*, Once we are *old* and full of *knowing* /a e / G a ...Fly...
3)We're *here* and gone this candle *flicker*,*Spinning* on a wheel that is larger than *life*/a e /G a
It's *hard* to know the bigger *picture*,To *understand* it all and be free from *strife* /ae/Ga...Fly...
4)Your gypsy *soul* it keeps you *moving*, Rolling all *around* like a *tumble* weed /a e / G a
You're fully *grown* but you're still *learning*, Learning what it *means* to be truly *free* /a e /G a
Rainbow Spirit Oregon (Groovy) a e G a : / istok.de/6650

18

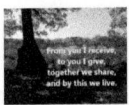

From You I Receive

From *you* i *receive*, To *you* i *give* (G C)(D G)
Together we *share*, And from *this* we *live* (G C)(D G)
Joseph And Nathan Segal (Jewish musical duo from
70's): / istok.de/6165

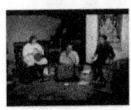

Ganesha Sharanam

//: *Ganesha* Sharanam *Sharanam Ganesha* :// C G C
//: *Ganesha* Sharanam Sharanam Ganesha :// G
//: *Ganesha* Sharanam Sharanam Ganesha :// C
Sahadev (Groovy)(Echo) Sharanam=surrender C G C G
C... / istok.de/6655

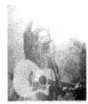

Ganga Ma

From The High Hima*layas*, To The *Plains* Far Below (e, D)
Carrying A *Message,* Singing *Sweetly* As You Flow (C D, e)
Flowing Free Flowing *Endlessly* (D) To The *Sea, Flowing* To The *Sea* (C, D e)
/: Jaia Ganga *Ma* Jaia Ganga *Ma*(eD) Jaia Ganga *Ma,Jai* Jai Ganga *Ma* :/(C,De)
Flowing Gliding Moving On, *Everlasting* Ever Strong (e, D)
Ganga Ma, You *Carry* Me Back *Home* (C, D e)
Take Me With You On Your Way, *Purifying* Each New Day (,D)
Ganga Ganga *Ma*, Ki Jaia *Jai* (C D, e) ...Jaia Ganga...
Murray Kyle: / istok.de/7573

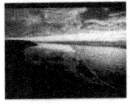

Gayatri Mantra

OM (a)
BHUR BHUVAH *SVAHA* (E a)
TAT SAVITUR, VARENYAM (E a, Ga)
BHARGO DEVASYA *DHIMAHI* (E C)
DHIYO YO NAH, *PRACHODAYAT* (F, Ga)
Tina Malia(E a)(E a, Ga)(E C)(F, Ga): / istok.de/5575-1

Deva Premal: / a / a / F G C / F G C - E / istok.de/5575-2

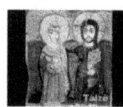

Gloria in Excelsis Deo

Gloria Gloria in Excelsis *Deo, Gloria Gloria Alleluia Alleluia* / a d G C, a d G C
Taize: a d G C / istok.de/5828

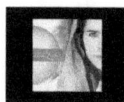

Gobindah Haray

//: *Gobindah Gobindah Haray* Haray ://: (8x) a e a
//: *Gobindah Gobindah Haray* Haray ://: (8x) C G a
Haray Haray Haray Haray Haray Haray Haray Haray ../a e a e..
Amrit Kirtan (1/3): istok.de/5870

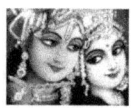

Gopala Devakinandana Gopala

//: *Gopala Gopala, Devakinandana Gopala* ://: (D A, G AD)
//: *Devakinandana* Gopala, *Devakinandana Gopala* ://: (D - G AD)
Krishna Das: / istok.de/6660-1

Jai Uttal: C e F G / istok.de/6660-2

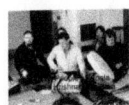 **Gopala Govinda Krishna Vasudeva**

//: *Gopala* Govinda Krishna vasudeva (a)
Radica Chandrika gouri Krishna *vasudeva* :// (d a)
//: *VASUDEVA, VASUDEVA, VASUDEVA* :// (CG, FC, a)
Bhajan People: a/ d a/ C G, F C a / istok.de/5622-1

 Kirtan Band: / istok.de/5622-2

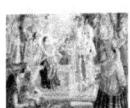 # Govinda Jai Jai

Govinda Jai Jai *Gopala Jai* Jai, Govinda Jai Jai *Gopala Jai* Jai (d a d, a d)
Radha Ramana Hari *Govinda Jai* Jai,Radha Ramana Hari Govinda *Jai* Jai(d a d,a d)
Chinmaya Dunster (Groovy): d a d, a d / istok.de/5825-1

 George Harrison(Groovy): G g D G / istok.de5825-2

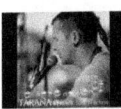 # Govinda Jaya Jaya

//: *Govinda Jaya* Jaya, *Gopala Jaya* Jaya :// a F, G a
//: Radha *Ramana* Hari, *Govinda Jaya* Jaya :// a F, G a

Govinda Govinda...Gopala Gopala...
Tarana & Friends(Groovy): g G or e E or d D / <u>istok.de/5852</u>

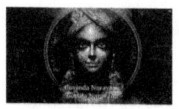

Govinda Narayana

Govinda narayana, *Gopala narayana; Govinda* narayana, *Gopala narayana* (d, C d);(d, C d)
//: *Govinda* Govinda, *narayana;Govinda* Govinda, *narayana* :// (d, Cd);(d, Cd)
(Hari) *Govinda Ananda, narayana* / F C, ad)
Master Reiki (Groovy): / <u>istok.de/6616-1</u>

Sivananda Chants Montreal Center (Groovy): / <u>istok.de/6616-2</u>

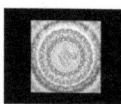

Govindam Adi Pursham

Govindam Adi P*urusham* Tam A*ham* B*hajami* (Dm Gm Bb C)
1)venum kvanantaravinda-dalayataksham (F Gm C Dm)
barhavatamsam asitam (Gm C) buda-sundarangam (C Dm)
kandarpa-kothi-kamaniya (Dm Gm F)-vis'esha s'obham (Bb A7)...govindam...
2)angani yasya sakalendriya-vrittimanti (F Gm Dm Gm F C)
pasyanti panti kalayanti ciram jaganti (Bb C Dm Bb)
ananda-cin-maya-saduj-jvala-vigrahasya (Dm F C Gm F)
//: govindam adi-purushamtam aham bhajami :// (C DmBb C)
George Harrison: / <u>istok.de/5787</u>

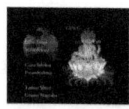

Guru Brahma

Guru Brahma (a (h) e) *Guru Vishnu* (a (h)e) Guru Devo *Maheshwara* (dE)
//: *Guru,* Sakshat,Parambrahma (H) Tasmai *Shree* Gura*ve* Nama*ha* (e d e)
Tasmai Shree Gura*ve* Nama*ha* :// (d E)
Deva Premal & Moten, Manose: / <u>istok.de/7563</u>

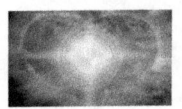

Guru Guru Wahe Guru

//: *Guru* Guru *Wahe* Guru, *Guru* Ram *Das* Guru :// (D A, Bm D G-A)
//: *Guru* Guru Wahe *Guru*, *Guru* Ram Das *Guru* :// (D C , G D-A)
Snatam Kaur (Echo): / istok.de/6572-1

 Amrit Kirtan: a G F, C G a F / istok.de/6572-2

 Meditative Mind: D, e C D / istok.de/6572-3

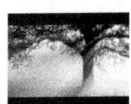

Guru Ram Das

//: Guru Guru Wahe Guru, *Guru Ramdas Guru* :// (C G a)(C G F)
//: *Ra Ma Da* Sa, *Sa Say So* Hung :// (C G a, C G F)
Mirabai Ceiba (Canon)(1/3): / istok.de/5738

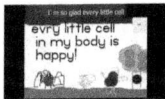

Happy and Well

Every little cell in my body is happy,Every little cell in my body is well(C, G C)
I'm so glad... *Every* little cell, In my body is *happy* and *well* (C, G C)
Karl Anthony: C...G-C / istok.de/6302

23

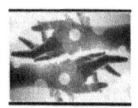

Har Hare Hari Wahe Guru

//: Har Hare Hari, *Wahe* Guru, *Har* Hare Hari *Wahe* Guru :// (a e, a e)
//: Har Hare Hari, *Wahe* Guru, *Har* Hare Hari *Wahe* Guru :// (a e, a G)
Gurudass Singh & Kaur (Groovy): a e a e... / istok.de/7078-1

Unknown: a C , G E / istok.de/7078-2

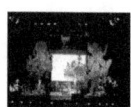

Hara Hara Amarnatha Gange

2x Hari Hari *amarnatha gange*, kashi *vishvanatha gange* (C F, G C)
2x Kashi *amarnatha* gange, kashi *vishvanatha gange* (C, F C)
2x Hari Hari *gautami gange*, kashi *vishvanatha gange* (C F, G C)
2x Kashi *gautami* gange, kashi *vishvanatha gange* (C, F C)
2x Hari, Hari *mahadeva shambo*, kashi *vishvanatha gange* (C F, G C)
2x Kashi *mahadeva* shambo, kashi *vishvanatha gange* (C, F C)
GAUTAMI GANGE . . . . . .*HARE*, HARE (C)
NARMADE, *JATA* SHANKARE, *PARVATI* PATE, *BOM* BOM (C)
Nina Hagen (Groovy)(Echo): C F G C, C F C, C... / istok.de/5634

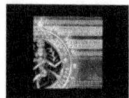

Hara Hara Guru Deva

Hara Hara Guru *Deva*, *Hara Hara* Guru *Deva* (G D e, G D e-C)
Para *Brahma* Para*meshvara*,*Para Brahma* Para*meshvara* (D e,C D e-G)
Hara *Hara*, Guru *Deva*, Hara *Hara*, Guru *Deva* (D e, G D e-C)
Robert Gass: / istok.de/5628

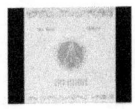

Hara Hara Mahadeva

/: *Hara* Hara Hara Hara Mahaadeva :/ (a)
/: *Shiva* Shiva Shiva Shiva Sadaa Shiva :/ (E)
/:Om *Hara* Hara Hara Hara Mahaadeva :/ 4x (a)
/:*Om* Namo Namo Namah Shiv*aaya*:/ 4x (d E)
//: *Brahma* Vishnu Surarchithaaya (a) *Om* Namo Namo Namah Shiv*aaya* :// (d E)
//: *Uma* Ganesha Sharavana Sevita (E) *Om* Namo Namo Namah Shivaaya :// (a)
//: *Om* Namo Namo Namah Shiv*aaya* :// 4x (d E)
Tina Malia and Shimshay: / <u>istok.de/7377</u>

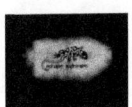

Hare Hare Om Namoh

//: Hare Hare *Om* Namoh, Hare Hare *Om* Namoh (aG)
Hare Hare *Om* Namoh, Hare hare *hare* :// (Ea)
//: *Om* Namo *Shivaya*, *Om* Namo Shivaya :// (a G, E a)
Satyaa & Pari (Groovy): a G E a / <u>istok.de/8200</u>

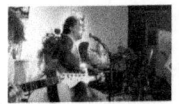

Hare Krishna (Maha Mantra)

Hare Krishna Hare Krishna (e) *Krishna* Krishna Hare Hare (e)
Hare Rama *Hare* Rama (C D) *Rama* Rama *Hare* Hare (D e)
Danilo Steinert (Groovy, Pure Power!): / <u>istok.de/8102-1</u>

Satyaa & Pari (Groovy): / <u>istok.de/8102-2</u>

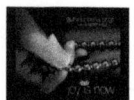

Hari Om

Hari *Om* Dear Lord (e) Sat *Nam* Holy Name (C)
When I *call* on the *Light* within (D C) *I go* home (e)
//:*Call* on the light within:// (e),(C) //:*Call* on the light:// (D),(C)
Call on the light within (e)
Solo: There's *Buddha*, Nanak, Allah too(a) *Jehovah*, Rama,and the true Guru (h)
Jesus, Moses and Vishnu (C) *Krishna*, Ram Das and the God in you (D)
Peace on Earth, good will to all (a) The *time* has come for us to stand tall (h)
Call on the Light that shines within (C) *Call* on the Light within (H7)
GuruGanesha Band Snatam Kaur / e C D C / istok.de/7398

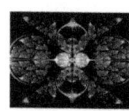

Hari Om Namoh Narayana

Hari *Om* Namoh *Narayana*, Om *Namoh* Narayana (a E)(E)
Hari *Om* Namoh *Narayana*,Hari *Om* Namoh *Narayana*(F a)(F a)
Deva Premal: / istok.de/5799

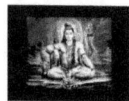

Hari Om Shiva Om

//: Hari *Om* Shiva *Om* Shiva *Om* Hari *Om* :// (d C, FC d)
//: Hari *Om* Shiva *Om* Shiva *Om* Hari *Om* :// (d F, C d)
Deva Premal (Groovy): / istok.de/6739

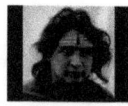

Hari Sharanam Shiva Sharanam

//: *Hari* Sharanam *Shiva Sharanam* :// a G a
//: *Shri* Ram Sharanam *Prabhu* Krishna *Sharanam* :// a G a

//: *Govinda* Jaya Jaya *Gopala Jaya* Jaya :// a G a
//: *Radha* Ramana Hare *Govinda Jaya* Jay :// a G a
Emanuele Lasorella (Groovy): / istok.de/7082

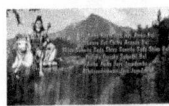

He Amba Bol

//: *He* Amba He Amba He Amba *Bol,Ishwara Sata* Chita *Ananda Bol* ://a d, a d Bb a
//: *(Sri) Sambasada* Shiva Sambasada Shiva Sambasada Shiva *Bol* / a d
Palaka Preraka Jaga* Pati *Bol* :// a d Bb a (*Satya-Tina Malia)
//: *Amba* Amba *Jaya Jagadamba* / a d a
Akhilandeshwari Jaya Jagadamba :// 4x d Bb(G)a
Mantra Salud (Groovy): / istok.de/7155-1

Tina Malia and Shimshay (Groovy): / istok.de/7155-2

Haidhakandi Bol (Ananda) (Groovy): ada, aEa, ada, aEa / istok.de/7155-3

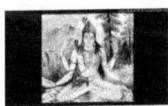

He Bhavani He Kalyani

//: *He* bhavani He kalyani, *He* maveshi*namo namah :// (a, d E a)*maheshwari
[/: *Shakti* durgani *namo* namah, *Shakti* bhavani *namo namah* :/] x2 (a E, a E a)
Adhyatman: a / d E a / a E / a E a / istok.de/5502

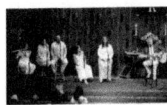

Heart of the Mother

I am *one* with the *heart* of the *Mother*, *I* am *one* with the *heart* of *Love* (adGC)
I am *one* with the *heart* of the *Father*, *I* am *one* with *God* (a d G E7)

27

Ave Maria Kyrie Eleison, Ave Maria Kyrie Eleison (a d G C, a d G E7)
Let me *remebmer Let* me *remember* (a d)
Let me *remember* I am *One* with *God* (G C (E7))
Ich bin eins mit dem Herzen der Mutter, Ich bin eins mit der Liebe (a d G C)
Ich bin eins mit dem Herzen des Vaters, Ich bin eins mit Gott (a d G E7)
Michael Stillwater, Seattle Unity Church: a d G C, a d G E7: <u>istok.de/5652-1</u>

Voices of the Heart: / <u>istok.de/5652-2</u>

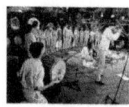

Heaven on Earth

//: Let the *heaven* be reflected by the *earth*, *Lord** (a E, a) - *Now
Let the *earth* may *turn* into *heaven* :// (G E a)
//: Let the *heaven* be *reflected* by the *earth*, *Lord* (d G C, a)
Let the *earth* may *turn* into *heaven* :// (d G E - e)
Reflecting heaven...Allah Hu Allah Hu.../ acapella
Christian Bollmann: / <u>istok.de/5840-1</u>

Gerhard Lipold: / <u>istok.de/5840-2</u>

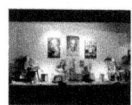

Heavenly Father let us adore Thee

1)Heavenly *Father*, let us *adore* Thee, Heaven and *earth* are full of Thy *glory*
All of *creation* repeats Thy *Name* ...*Halleluya*
2)Heavenly *Mother* of Power and *Beauty*, To love and to *serve* Thee is *our* Blessed duty
All of *creation* obeys Thy *name* ... *Halleluya* ... //: Halle*luya*, Hallelu Hallelu-*ya* ://
3)Heavenly *Master* of Wisdom and *Kindness*, Rescue Thy *children* from darkness and *blindness*
All of *creation* will follow Thy *Name* ... *Halleluya*
4)Brothers and *Sisters* in Love come *together*, with strength of the *spirit* no sorrow can *sever*
All of *creation* is our eternal *home* ... *Halleluya*... //: Halle*luya*, Hallelu Hallelu-*ya* ://
Janin Devi: C a C a C a... / <u>istok.de/6335</u>

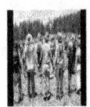

Here We Are Once Again

Here we *are* once again, holding *hands* in a *circle* (a G, a)
And the *love* that we share, shining *out* all over the *world* (a G, a)
People of the world are now *awakening*, *Feels* like we've *all* been here *before* (a G a, a G a)
Remember the love *remember* that *power*, We thought we *lost* so long *ago* (a G a, a G a)
//: Let love *rain*, let it rain, let love *rain* all over the *world* :// 4x (a, G a) Freedom, freed...
Rainbows: a G a, a G a ... / istok.de/6283

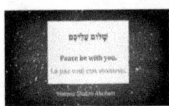

Hevenu shalom aleychem

Hevenu *shalom* aleychem, Hevenu *shalom* aleychem (a, d)
Hevenu *shalom* a*leychem*, Hevenu *shalom* shalom shalom a*leychem* (Ea,E a)
Es werde Frieden auf Erden, Es werde Frieden auf Erden
Es werde Frieden auf Erden, Es werde Frieden Frieden Frieden auf der Welt
The Brooklyn Tabernacle Choir: a, d, E a, E a / istok.de/5636

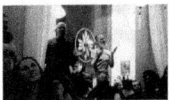

Hey Niketi Hey Wana

Hey Niketi Hey Wana, *Hey* Niketi Hey Wana / a, G
Asey Wana *Hey* Wana, *Asey* Wana *Hey* Wana / a d, E a
1)*Hey* Brother Hey Sister, *Wherever* You come from Wherever You go to /a,G
We All Are *connected*, *Forever* in Our *Hearts* / a d, E a ...Hey Nikitey...
2)*Hej* Bruder Hej Schwester, *Egal* wo Du herkommst Egal wo Du hingest /a,G
Wir sind *verbunden*, Für *immer* von Herz zu *Herz* / a d, E a ...Hey Nikitey...
Tuulia and Healing Chants Family (Groovy): / istok.de/7223

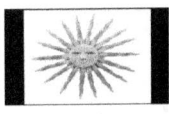

Hey Shiva Shankara Hey Maheshvara

//: *Hey* Shiva Shankara *Hey Maheshvara* :// (a E a)
//: *Chica* Hara Chica Dhara *Hara* Hara *Shankara* :// (a F E)

29

Om Namaha Shiva Hare *Om* Namaha Shiva (E a)
Nina Hagen (Groovy): a E a, a E a, a F E, E a / istok.de/5643

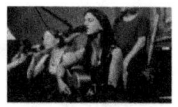

Hi Henej Manej Ya

Hi Henej Manej Ya Hi Henej Manej Ya,Hi Henej Mana o *ey /a,E*
Yvonne Seelensängerin: a E a E a... / istok.de/5838

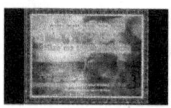

Hiney ma tov uma nayim

//:*Hiney* ma tov uma *nayim,shevet* achim *gamyachad* ://(dg,A7d)
Hiney ma tov, shevet achim *gamyachad* (d (C)F, g A7)
Hiney ma tov, shevet achim gamyachad (d (C)F, g A d)
Aschat (1/3) d g A7 d, d (C)F, g A7-d: / istok.de/5648

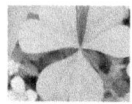

Hooponopono

I am *sorry* Plaese *forgive* me, I *thank* you And I *love* you / C a, d G
These are the *special* words, *God* send to us *all* / C a, d G
These are the *magic* words, *God* gave to us *all* / C a, d G
Hooponopono, *Hooponopono* / Ca, dG
Aman Ryuseke Seto: C a d G / istok.de/5831

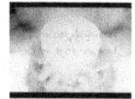

How could anyone

How Could *Anyone* Ever *Tell* You,You Are *Anything* Less Than *Beautiful*/dG,Ca
How Could *Anyone* Ever *Tell* You, You Were *Less* Than *Whole* / d G, C a - A7

How Could *Anyone* Fail To *Notice*, That Your *Loving* Is A *Miracle* / d G, C a
(And) How *Deeply* You're *Connected*, To My *Soul* / d G, C a - A7
Written: Libby Roderick Singer: Elaine Silver: / <u>istok.de/6586</u>

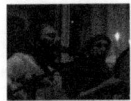

Hu Allah Allah Hu Allah

Let my *heart reflect* Thy *light* Lord / e H7 e
As the *moon reflects* the *light* of the *sun* / e H7 e H7
In love, Always in love / e H7 e...
Hu Allah, Allah *Hu Allah*, *Hu Allah*, Allah Hu... / e H7 e H7...
KirtanUniversal: / <u>istok.de/6364</u>

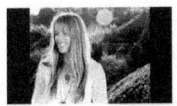

Hu Allah Hu

//: *Hu* Allah Hu Allah Si Leila Ha Illahua (a)
Hu Allah Hu Allah Si *Leila* Ha Illahua :// (d E)
//: *Hu* Allah Hu Allah Si Leila Ha Illahua (d C)
Hu Allah Hu Allah Si *Leila* Ha Illahua :// (G E)
Deva Premal (Groovy): / <u>istok.de/5807</u>

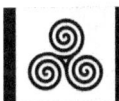

I am a Circle

I am a circle, *I* am healing you (d,C)
Y*ou* are a circle, You are healing *me (d,C)*
Unite us, *be* one, *Unite* us, be as *one* (d, C, d, C)
Ky's recording: (d, C) / <u>istok.de/6134</u>

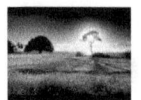

I Am A Walking Tree

I am a walking tree *You* are a walking tree, I am a walking tree You are a walking tree
Feet on the *earth-head* in the *sky* //: My *heart* joins *together* The *two* to one to *see* :// *I..*
/: Bringing the light *down Into* the darkest *ground, Releasing* the *dark* side *Into* the *light* :/
Variations: I *breathe* in what you *breathe* out, You *breathe* in what I breathe *out*
Breath is connecting us *all*, Love is connecting us *all*
Light is connecting us *all*, As the *moon* Mirrors the *sun*
Let our *lives* Mirror the *one*, *Source* of all Light of *love*
As the *stars* Are gateways To *eternity*, Let this *moment* Be the *key* To be free
This *moment* Is the *key*...!
Kailash: d C d C... or: a G a G... / istok.de/6594

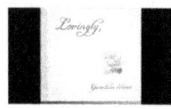

I am the Light of the Soul

//: I am the light of the soul, I am *bountiful* (a, e)
 I am *beautiful* I am bliss, I am I *am* :// (F, E)
//: I am the light of the *soul*, I am *bountiful*, (F G, a)
I am *beautiful*, I am *bliss*, I am, I *am* :// (G, F, E)
Gurudass Kaur (1/3): / istok.de/6719-1

Gurudass Kaur (1/3) (Faster): / istok.de/6719-2

Ajeet Kaur: C G F, C G e-F, C G F / istok.de/6719-3

Sirgun Kaur & Sat Darshan Singh: A G D... / istok.de/6719-4

32

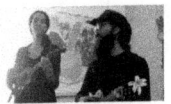

I Find my Joy in the Simple Things

I *Find* My Joy In The *Simple* Things, *Coming* From The *Earth*
I *Find* My Joy In The *Sun* That Shines, And The *Water* That *Sings* To Me
//: *Listen* To The Wind And *Listen* To The Water, *Hear* What They *Say* ://
....Singing *Heya* Heya *Heya* Heya *Heya* Heya *Ho* (x4)
//: Let *Us* Never *Forget* Never *Forget* To Give *Thanks* :// Singing Heya...
//: Give *Thanks* Give *Thanks* Give *Thanks* And *Praise* :// Singing Heya
WahRho: a C G a / istok.de/6613

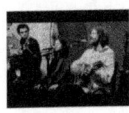

I Just Close My Eyes (The River)

//: *I* Just Close My *Eyes* (e h)
And The *World* Is Carried *Away* By The *River* :// (a h e)
//: *What* Is Left *Behind* I Can't *Say* (Cmaj7 h a)
It's Just The *Sound* Of *Water* :// (h e)
Uria Tsur: A: Bm/A/G/F#m/Bm / B: Em/F#m/G/A/Bm/ istok.de/7311-1

Deva Madhuro: / istok.de/7311-2

Thilo Martinho: / istok.de/7311-3

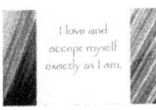

I love and accept myself

I *love* and *accept* myself, *Exactly* as I *am* / C F, C G
I *love* and *accept* myself, *All* is well *in* my world / F C, F C

33

All is well *in* my world , *OM* / F C, FG
Ananda: / istok.de/6325

Ich bin das pure Licht

//: Ich *bin* das pure Licht, Mit *Liebe flut'* ich *Dich* :// (a G e a)
//: Ich bin die pure Liebe, Und das *Licht* sind *meine Flügel* :// (G e a)
//: Die Schmerzen lass sie *gehen*,Und *Wahrheit* wirst du *sehen*://(G,ea)
//: Die Liebe lass sie *frei*, Und sie *kommt* bei Dir *vorbei* :// (G, e a)
Rainbows (Groovy): (a G - E) or (a G e a) / istok.de/7286-1

Viola on harp: / istok.de/7286-2

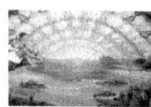

Ide Were Were

Ide *Were* Were *Nita Oshun*, Ide *Were* Were / a G C, a
Ide *Were* Were *Nita Oshun*, Ide *Were* Were *Nitaya* / a G C, a F
Oche *Kiniba* Nita *Oshun*, *Cheke* Cheke *Cheke* / F G, C F
Nitaya, Ide *Were Were* / G, E-E7
Deva Premal: / istok.de/7307

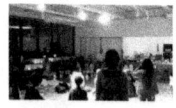

In the Heart Arunachala

In the *Heart Arunachala* (C) (a)
This is *Shiva* This is *Shankara* (d) (G7)
In the *Heart Arunachala* (C) (a)
This is *Shiva* This is *Ramana* In the *Heart* (d) (G7) (C)

34

Bhogi Yogi Ananda Expless: / istok.de/7383-1

 Ramanai: / istok.de/7383-2

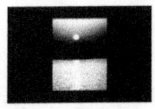 **In the Still of the Night**

1)In the *still* of the night (e)
From the *darkness* comes the *light* (C e)
//: And I *know* in my *heart* it is *you* :// (C D e)
2)When the *truth* is revealed (e)
All the *sorrows* will be *healed* (C e) ...//: And I *know* ...
3)When the *fire* in my soul (e)
Burns the *longing* for a *goal* (C e) ...//: Than I *know*...
Jai *Ma*, Jai *Ma*...Jai Jai *Ma*...
Rainbows (famous Amma Bhajan): / istok.de/7536

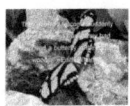 **Ishq Allah Mahbud Lillah**

//: *Ishq*-allah Mah-*bud*-lillah (A E)
Ishq-allah Mah-*bud*-lillah :// (f# D)
Allah Ya Ja*mil* (A f#) *Allah* Ya Ka*rim* (D A)
Allah Ya Ra*him* (f# h) *Allah Allah* (E A)
Sudha (1/3): God (I am) is Love Lover and Beloved / istok.de/7542-1

 Deva Premal: / istok.de/7542-2

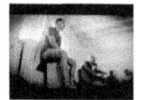

It's The Heartbeat Of The Universe

It's The *Heartbeat* Of The Universe (h)
It's The *Silence In* Your *Soul* (G A h)
It's The *Joy* That Makes Every Moment New (h)
It's The *Bliss* When *We* Are *Whole* (G A h)
Om *Shanti*, Om *Shanti*, Shanti *Om* (A, G, h)
Johannes Vogt (Om Shanti): / istok.de/14012

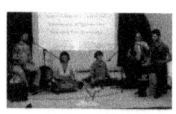

Jago Ma

//: *Jago* Ma Jago Ma *Shankari Ma* :// (d7 G d7)
//: *Shankari Ma* Aba*yankari* Ma :// (d7 A7 d7)
//: *Devi* Da*ya* Karo Shiva Rama*na* :// (d7 G d7)
Satyananda Yoga Kirtan Csoport (Groovy dark): / istok.de/7560

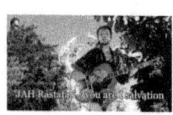

Jah Rastafari You are my salvation

/: *Jah Rastafari* You are my *salvation*, You help I *realise*
That *Love* is surrounding us *all*, In Every *Situation* Here With *I* and I:/
//: *Let* the Music *Free* Your Soul, *Great* Spirit is in *Full* Control ://
//: Oh *Jah* You Have Given *Me*, Everything I *Need,*
To Be *Free*, In This *Reality, In This Reality* ://
//: Lieber *Gott*, Du hast mir *gegeben*, Alles was ich *brauch*
In diesem *Leben*, um *frei* zu sein, um *frei* zu sein ://
Shimshai & Jah Levi: a G a G a G... / istok.de/8109-1

Shimshai with Assi Rose: / istok.de/8109-2

36

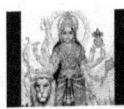

Jai Ambe Jagadambe

/: *Jai* Ambe *Jagad-ambe*, *Mata Bhavuman Jai* Ambe :/ (eDe,GDe)
/: *Durga* Vinashini *Durga* Jai Jai, *Kala* Vinashini *Kali* Jai Jai :/ (eG,De)
/:*Uma* Rama Brah*mani* Jai Jai, *Radha* Rukamani *Sita* Jai Jai :/ (DG,De)
Everhigh: / <u>istok.de/5654</u>

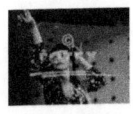

Jai Bajaranga Bali Jai Hanuman Ki

//: *Jay Bhajarangabali*, Jay Hanuman *Ki* :// (a G)(a)
/:Jay Mahavira *Jay* Hanuman,*Jay* Gurudeva Karo *Kalyan*:/(G)(e a)
Nina Hagen (Groovy): a d G a / <u>istok.de/7210-1</u>

Shaktipriya (Groovy): / <u>istok.de/7210-2</u>

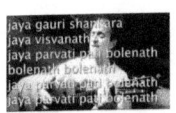

Jai gauri Shankara

//: *Jai* gauri shankara Jai vishvanath, Jai parvati pati *bhole nath* ://(C, GC)
//: *Bhole* nath, *bhole nath* ; *Bhole* nath, *bhole nath* (C, FC ; C FC)
Jai parvati pati *bhole* nath, *Jai* parvati pati *bhole* nath :// (G C, G C)
Stefano Abbattista: / <u>istok.de/5661</u>

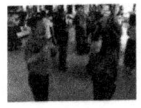

Jai Hanuman Jai Sitaram

//: *Jai* Hanuman *Jai* Jai *Hanuman* :// (a d a)

//: *Jai* Sitaram Jai *Jai* Sitaram :// (d E)
Dance of Universal Peace: a d a, d E / istok.de/5631

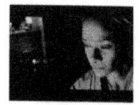

Jai Mata Kali Jai Mata Durge

//: *Jai* Mata Kali *Jai* Mata *Durge* :// (a E a)
//: *Kali* Durge *Namo Namah* :// (a E a)
//: *Kali* Durge *Namo Namah* :// (d a)
//: *Kali* Durge *Namo Namah* :// (a E a)
Nina Hagen, Moti Maa (Groovy): / istok.de/5846

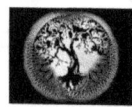

Jai Radha Madhava

//: *Jai* Radha *Madhava, Jai* Kunja *Vihari* :// (a C)(G a)
//: *Jai* Gopi Jana *Vallabha, Jai* Gire *Balihari* ://(C a)(G a)
Deva Premal: / istok.de/5729-1

Jagjit Singh: / istok.de/5729-2

Manish Vyas: / istok.de/5729-3

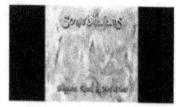

Jamna Ki Jai Jai

Jamna ki jai jai, *Ganga* ki *jai* jai / x2 (a, d a)

38

Kailasha Shakti Shiva, *Shankara* ki *jai* jai / x2 (a, E a)
Baba ki jai Bhole, *Baba* ki *jai* jai / x2 (a, d a)
Kailasha Shakti, Haidya*khandi* ki *jai* jai / x2 (a, E a)
Govinda jai jai, *Gopala jai* jai / x2 (a, d a)
Radha Ramana Hari, *Govinda jai* jai / x2 (a, E a)
Somebhajans (Groovy): a d a, a E a: / <u>istok.de/5849</u>

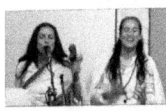

Jay Ganga Ma

//: *Jay* Ganga Jay Ganga Jay Ganga *Ma* :// x4 a G
//: Jay Ganga *Ma* Jay Ganga *Ma* :// x4 a G
//: *Amma* Amma Amma, Jay ganga *Ma* :// x4 a G
//: Jay Ganga Ma Jay Ganga *Ma* :// x4 a G
Sangeeta (Groovy, Echo): a G a G a... / <u>istok.de/6631-1</u>

 Ganga Mira (Groovy): a G a G ... / <u>istok.de/6631-2</u>

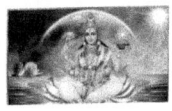

Jay Ganga Ma Oh Ma

Jay ganga *Ma* Jay ganga *Ma* Oh *Ma* / F C
Jay ganga *Ma* Jay ganga *Ma* Oh *Ma* / d A
Jay ganga *Ma* Jay ganga *Ma* Oh *Ma* / d F
Jay *Mata* Ganga Jai *Ma* / C A7
Marie Gabriella & Nicole Salmi: / <u>istok.de/6619-1</u>

 Rishkesh: / <u>istok.de/6619-2</u>

Nicole Salmi(On the beach in Brasil):/ istok.de/6619-3

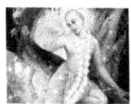

Jay Shree Krishna Chaitanya

Jai Sri *Krishna* Chaitanya, Prabhu Nityan*andana* (a, d)
Hare Krishna Hare Ram, *Radhe* Govindam (e, a)
Namaste: a d e a / istok.de/6729

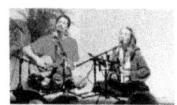

Jay Shri Ma

//: *Jay* Shri *Ma* (e G) Kali Kali *Ma* (a) Jay Shri *Ma* :// (e)
//: *Ananda* Ma *Durga* Devi (G D) *Jagadambe* Shri *Ma* :// (a e)
Janin Devi: / istok.de/8105

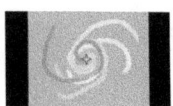

Jaya Bhagavan

Jaya Bhaga*van*,Jaya Bhaga*van*(A,e) Jaya Bhaga*van*,*Jaya* Bhaga*van*(C, D A)
Jaya Bhaga*van*,Jaya Bhaga*van*(G,C) Jaya Bhaga*van*,*Jaya* Bhaga*van*(G,D A)
Tina Malia and Shimshai: / istok.de/7503-1

Krishna Das: / istok.de/7503-2

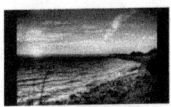

Jaya Jaya Devi Mata

Jaya Jaya, Devi Mata, Namaha (a e, a e, aGa)
Jaya Jaya, Devi Mata, Namaha (a e, a e, aGa)
Henry Marshall (Canon): / istok.de/8122-1

 Sarva Antah with children: / istok.de/8122-2

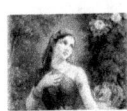

Jaya Radha Jaya Madhava

Jaya Radha *Jaya* Madhava,Jay Govinda *Jay* Gopala /a d, a
Jaya Radhe! Jaya Radhe, Hare Krishna, *Hare* Hare / E, a
(Mukunda Madhava *Hare* Murare)
Jai Uttal: / istok.de/5768

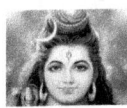

Jaya Shiva Omkara

//: *Jaya* Shiva *Omkara* (ae) *Jaya* Shiva *Omkara* (Ga) ://4x
//: *Mahadevaya* Maheswar*aya* (aGea)
Mahadevaya Maheswaraya (aGea) :// ...Jaya...
//: Sri Yog*eshwara* Jaya Jaga*dishwara* (aG)
Mata Pri*tatuma* He Yog*eshwara)* (e a) :// ...+2x Mata...
Bittu Mallick (Echo): also: (e h) (D e) , (e D) (h
e) / istok.de/8127-1

41

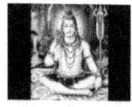 Manish Vyas (Groovy, Echo): / <u>istok.de/8127-2</u>
2x low 2x high: //: Jaya *Jaya* Shiva Om*kara* (e h)
Hare *Hare* Hara Om*kara* (C De) ://

Jaya Shiva Shankara boom boom Hare Hare

//: *Jaya* Shiva *Shankara Om* Om *Hare* Hare :// a G C E
//: *Hare* Hare *Hare* Hare *Om* Om *Hare* Hare :// a G C E
Namaste: a G C E / <u>istok.de/6231</u>

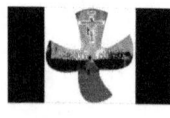

Jesus remember me

Jesus remember me *when* You come in to Your *Kingdom* (a d G C)
Jesus remember me *when* You come in to Your *Kingdom* (a d G C)
Taize: a d G C / <u>istok.de/5665-1</u>

 Ananda (1/3): / <u>istok.de/5665-2</u>

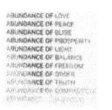

Join Hands

Join *hands* in the *circle*, Of *abundance* and *love* / Ca, Fe
We are *blessed* and we *prosper*, Wherever we *turn* / Ce, FG
We *receive* what we *want*, And we *share* what we *can*/CG,aF
Join *hands* in the *circle*, Of *abundance* and *love* / Cd, FC

Ananda: / istok.de/6318

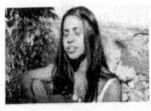

Jurema oh Jurema

//: Tava na *mata* com minha flecha na *mao* / d C
e Mamae *Jurema* dentro do meu *coracao* :// A d
//: E la na *mata* encontrei *Tupinamba* / d C
E la na Jurema para vir me *acompanhar* :// A d
...*Jurema* Oh *Jurema, Jurema* Oh *Jurema* / d C A d
//: Foi la na *mata* que encontrei a *inspiracao* / d C
para eu *seguir* no caminho do *coracao* :// A d ...Jurema Oh...
//: *Cabocla* Jurema, Cabocla *Guerreira* / d C
Oh Jurema, Feiticeira :// A d....Jurema Oh Jurema
Josii Yakecan: d C A d / istok.de/7291

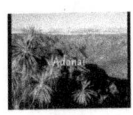

Kadosh Adonai

[//: *Kadosh Kadosh Kadosh* :// a d a
//: *Adonai Elohim tzevaot* ://] 2x G e a
[//: *Asher hayah vehoveh veyavo* ://] 2x A G D A
Elisheva Shomron: / istok.de/6278-1

Barry & Batya Segal: / istok.de/6278-2

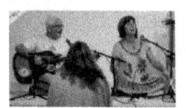

Kali Maha Durge Ma

//: *Kali* Kali Maha Kali, *Kali* Durge *Ma* :// (a, d E)
//: *Kali* Kali Maha Kali, *Kali* Durge *Ma* :// (a, d E)
Mudita Group (Groovy): a, d E / istok.de/5514

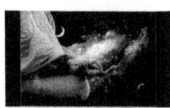

Kodoish Kodoish Kodoish Adonai Tsebayoth

Kodoish Kodoish Kodoish Adonai Tsebayoth (a)
Kodoish Kodoish Kodoish *Adonai Tsebayoth* (E a)
Metatron: a E a / istok.de/6263

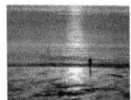

Kuate leno leno maote

Kuate leno leno maote, Hayeno Hayeno Hayeno (a, G a)
We are as One in the infinite Sun /(Let me be One with infinite Sun)(a)
Forever Forever Forever (G a)
Christian Bollmann, acapella or: a G a / istok.de/5669

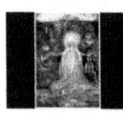

Lady Of The Flowing Waters

Lady of the *shining stars*, *Lady of* the *moonlight* (a C G e, a C G e)
Lady of the *dew* wet *dawn*, *Lady of* the *twilight* (a C G e, a C G e)
The *Goddess is* in *everything*, In *every form* of *nature* (C G a, a G a)
The *Goddess is* in *everything* , In *every form* of *beauty* (C G a, a G a)
Lady of the *flowing waters*, *Lady of* the *mountain* (a C G e, a C G e)
Lady of the *flowing meadow*, *Lady of* the *forest* (a C G e, a C G e)
The Goddess is...The Goddess is... / Goddes Goddess

Robert Gass (1/3): a C G e / C G a, a G a / <u>istok.de/5671</u>

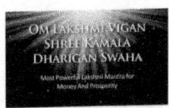

Lakshmi Mantra

Om Lakshmi Vigan Shree Kamala Dharigan Swaha (a) / (e)
Om Lakshmi Vigan Shree Kamala *Dharigan Swaha*(F G e) /(C D h)
Spoken: //: Om Lakshmi Vigan Shree Kamala Dharigan Swaha ://
Om Lakshmi Vigan Shree *Kamala* Dharigan Swaha (a F) / (e C)
Om Lakshmi Vigan Shree *Kamala Dharigan* Swaha (G F) / (D C)
Vayanamasi: / <u>istok.de/5740-1</u>

Kira Mantra: low: a G e a-e,high: d C a G-a/ <u>istok.de/5740-2</u>

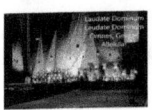

Laudate Dominum

Laudate Dominum, Laudate Dominum / a E, a G
Omnes Gentes, Alleluia / C G, F E7
Taize: / <u>istok.de/6629</u>

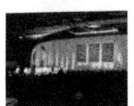

Laudate Omnes Gentes

Laudate Omnes Gentes, Laudate Dominum / C G a, F G
Laudate Omnes Gentes, Laudate Dominum / C G a, F C
Taize: / <u>istok.de/6626</u>

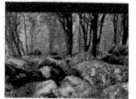

Let the circle be open

May the *circle* be open *but unbroken* (a E a)
May the *peace* of the Goddes be *ever* in your *heart* (a E a)
Mary mee and *mary part*,And *mary meet again*(C E a, C E a)
Robert Gass: / istok.de/5675

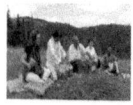

Listen Listen Listen To My Heart Song

//: *Listen* listen listen,To *my* heart*song* :// (e)(C G)
//: I will *always* love you, I will *always* serve you :// (G)(C)
//: I will *never* forget you, I will *never* forsake you :// (G)(C)
Shakti Deva: e C G , G C G C / istok.de/6149-1

Robert Gass: e C G , G C G C / istok.de/6149-2

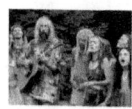

Live Your Heart Song

//: *Live* your heart song people, *People live* your heart *song* :// / F / F C F
'Cause we're *one* in the *spirit*, As we're *many* in the *flesh* / F C / Bb C
And when in *truth* flesh and *spirit* , *Realize* the union both are *blessed* / F C / Bb C
REF: So let me *play* let me *sing*, Let me *do* just what I'm *feeling* / F C / Bb C
And let you *play* let you *sing*, Let you *do* just what you're *feeling* / F C / Bb C
//: *Live* your heart song people, *People live* your heart *song* :// / F / F C F
2)And the *truth* the whole *truth*,And nothing *but* the truth Is all that *stands* /FC/BbC
When all *of the misunderstandings*,Have been *resolved* And Illusions dissolve *away*...So let..
3)As the *Great* Mystery of life *Keeps* revealing itself,History *keeps unravelling* /F C /Bb C
Though a *few* have supressed the *many*,Now the *season* for release and *healing* /F C /Bb C
Rainbow Spirit Oregon: / istok.de/6648

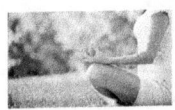

Lokah Samastah Sukhino Bhavantu

Lokah Samastah Sukhino Bhavantu (C a F C)
Om Shanti Shanti Shanti (by Deva Premal)
Sun Vaz: C a F C / istok.de/6477-1

 Deva Premal: a e G a , a G e a / istok.de/6477-2

 Wah!: e C 4x / a (h)-C / 4x / istok.de/6477-3

 Jane Winthers: a e a e... istok.de/6477-4

 Simone Vitale: C a C a C a...(with Echo) / istok.de/6477-5

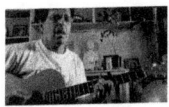

Love Love Love Love

Love love *love* love, *People* we are *made* for love (a G)(a E)
Love each other *as* ourselves, For *we* are *one* (a G)(a E7)
Act on Wisdom (Melody: Spann den Wagen): / istok.de/6228-1

Dear friends *Dear* friends, *Let* me tell you *how* I feel
You have given *me* such treasures, *I* love you so

47

Plum Village (Melody: Spann den Wagen): d C d a - A7 / istok.de/6228-2

Hey Du *vertraue* Deiner Kraft, *Wegen* ihr hast *Du* schon viel gemacht.
Liebe Lust und *Leben*, *Liebe* Lust und *Leben*

Relaxon: d C d a - A7 / istok.de/6228-3

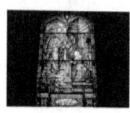

Magnificat Anima Mea Dominum

Magnificat Magnificat (a d G C)
Magnificat anima *mea Dominum* (a d G C)
Magnificat Magnificat Magnificat anima *mea* (a d G C)
Taize: a d G C (Meine Seele preist den Herrn!) / istok.de/5680

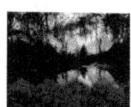

Mangalacharan

Om Om 4x (e h)
1)*Sarveshaam* swastir *bhavatu*, *Sarveshaam* shantir *bhavatu* (e h)(e h)
Sarveshaam poornam *bhavatu*,*Sarveshaam mangalam bhavatu*(G D)(Che)
2)*Sarve* bhavantu *sukhinah*, *Sarve* santu *niraamayaah* (e h)(e h)
Sarve bhadraani *pashyantu*, Maakaschit duhkha *bhaag bhavet* (G D)(Che)
Seven: Sacred Chants of Ancient India 3: / istok.de/7091

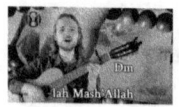

Mashallah Through your eyes

Through your eyes shines the Light / a

48

Mash'Allah Mash'Allah, *Wonder* of *god* in *you* / a, G e a
Mash'Allah Mash'Allah, *Mash'Allah Mash'Allah* / C d, G a
Mash'Allah Mash'Allah, *Wonder* of *god* in *you* / C d, E a
Wonder of *god* in *you* / E E7 a... Through your eyes ...

Written by James Burgess sings Stefan Pulsaris
(Groovy): / istok.de/6598-1

Philipp Stegmüller (Groovy): / istok.de/6598-2

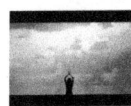

May the Long Time Sun Shine Upon You

May the long time sun (C G a) / (D A h)
Shine upon you (F C) / (G D)
All Love surround you (H F G) / (C G A)
And the pure Light (C G a) / (D A h)
within you (F C) / (G D)
Guide your way home (H F C) / (C G D)
Guide your way home (H F G) / (C G A)
Snatam Kaur (Sufi chant) / istok.de/6153

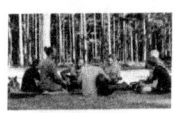

May the Love We're Sharing

May the *love* we're sharing *spread* its wings, And fly across the earth (a)
And bring new *joy* to every *soul*, Who is *alive* (G e, a)
May the blessings of your grace My love, Shine on everyone
And may we *all* see the light *within*, Within *within* (G e, a)
Salaam *Aleikum*, Aleikum-a-Salaam(3x)
...Hare *Krishna*, Krishna Krishna Hare (3)...Hallelujah...
(each 4th time): May *all* the beings in all the *worlds*, be *happy* (G, a)
Rainbows (Groovy): a G e a: / istok.de/7679-1

Healing Circles by Moving Breath: / <u>istok.de/7679-2</u>

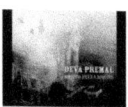

Moola Mantra

Om *Sat* Chit Ananda Parabrahma (a)
Purushothama Paramatma (a)
Sri *Bhagavathe* Sameta (d)
Sri *Bhagavathe Namah* (G Fa)
Hari *Om* Tat Sat (a) (Hari Om...-Only by Deva and Seven)
Hari *Om* Tat Sat(G) Hari *Om* Tat *Sat*(F G) Hari *Om* Tat *Sat* (ea)
Deva Premal: a d G F a , a G F-G e a / <u>istok.de/5790-1</u>

Terry Oldfield: e a e h , C h a e / <u>istok.de/5790-2</u>

Bhakti Music(Groovy): aGa , aGC, CdGC, aGa / <u>istok.de/5790-3</u>

Unknown, Groovy : a E a , F G F a / <u>istok.de/5790-4</u>

Felicity Barrington: A D A D A D /e C D e C D / <u>istok.de/5790-5</u>

Yogini: C a C a C a... / <u>istok.de/5790-6</u>

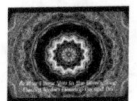

Mother I Feel You

//: Mother I feel you under my feet, Mother I hear your heartbeat ://
...Heya heya heya yah heya heya ho, Heya heya heya heya heya ho
//: Mother I hear you in the River song, eternal waters flowing on and on ://...Heya
//: Father I see you when the Eagle flies, Light of the Spirit going to take us higher ://
Windsong Martin (Groovy): A E A E... / <u>istok.de/5549</u>

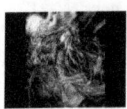

Mother of Darkness Chant

Mother of darkness Mother of light,*Earth beneath* us *souls* in flight /d, F C d
Songs of love and love of life, *Guide* us *through* our *hearts* / d, F C d
Alice Di Micele: <u>istok.de/6378</u>

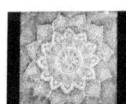

Mother of my Heart

//: *Mother* Of My Heart *Mother* Of My Soul (GD)
Sweet Mother Mary She's Calling Us Home :// (C)
-She Said You Are *Ready* Now, You Are *Ready* Now, You Are *Ready* Now (Oh My Sweet Child)
Holy Now You Are *Holy Now* //: *Take* My *Hand*, Take My Hand :// (G D C) (G -D- C)
-We'll Walk This Together //: Let *Go* Of This Illusion This *Fear* Of Separation (,G D)
There Is *Nothing* That Can Hold You, From The Light That You Are :// (C)
That You *Are*, Ho That You *Are* (G -D- C)
//: *All* The Love This Day, *All* The Love This *Way* (All The Love) :// (G, D C)
//: Love Is The *Key*, Turn It And *See*, Cause *Jah* Jah (Holy Spirit)* (G, D, C)
Is Right Here Inside Of *You* :// (*2nd time: Almighty) (G)
Pachamama Church: GD-C or CG-F / <u>istok.de/7580</u>

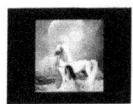

Mul Mantra

Ek Ong Kar, Sat Nam / d C F, h d
Kartaa *Purkh* Nirbhao *Nirvair* / C d

51

Akaal Moorat, Ajoonee / C F, h d
Saibhang, *Gur* Prasaad *Jap* / C d
Aad Sach, *Jugaad Sach, Hai* Bhee *Sach* / C F, h d, C d
Nanak Hosee *Bhee* Sach / h A
Amrit Kirtan (Mool Mantra): / <u>istok.de/7431-1</u>

Snatam Kaur (Groovy): d a C G d / high: A# d a d / <u>istok.de/7431-2</u>

GuruGanesha Band (Groovy): / C G d 4x / F G a - F G E E7 / <u>istok.de/7431-3</u>

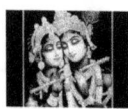

Murali Krishna

/: *Murali* Krishna Mukunda Krishna,Mohana Krishna *Krishna Krishna*:/(a E a)
//: *Gopi* Krishna Gopala Krishna, Govardhanadhara *Krishna Krishna* ://(a d a)
//: *Radha* Krishna Bala Krishna, Rasa Vilola *Krishna Krishna* :// (a E a)
//: *Shirdi* Krishna Parthi Krishna, Sri Sathya Sai *Krishna Krishna* :// (a d a)
Dana Gilespie: / <u>istok.de/5691</u>

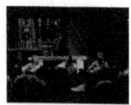

Music Of Silence

//: *Music* Of *Silence*, *Music* Beyond *Words* (G a, G a)
Children Of The *Ocean*, Thats What We *Are* :// (d e, a
-A7)
//: *Love* Is The Most *Shining* Star (d G)
In The Inner Sky Of Your Being (C a)
Love Is The Most *Shining* Star, *Inside* You :// (d e, a -A7)
Jay Jay Jay: / <u>istok.de/7670</u>

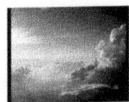

My peace

My *Peace* I *Leave* you (a d) My *Peace* I *Give* you (G C)
Trouble not your *hearts* (F E)
My *Peace* I *Leave* you (a d) My *Peace* I *Give* you (G C)
Be not *afraid* (F a)
Taize: / istok.de/7411

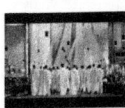

Nada te turbe

Nada te *turbe*, *Nada* te *espante* / (a d, G C)
Quien a Dios *tiene*, *Nada* le *falta* / (a F, E a)
Nada te *turbe*, *Nada* te *espante* / (a d, G C)
Solo Dios, *Basta* / (a F, Ea)
Taize: / istok.de/7108

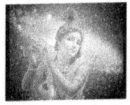

Narayana Narayana Jai Jai Govinda Hare

[//: *Narayana* Narayana Jai Jai Govinda *Hare* (d a)
Narayana Narayana Jai Jai *Govinda Hare* ://] 4x (C a d)
//: Jai Jai *Govinda Hare*, Jai Jai *Gopala* Hare :// (d a, d)
//: Jai Jai *Govinda Hare*, Jai Jai *Gopala* Hare :// (d G)
//: Jai Jai *Govinda Hare*, Jai Jai *Gopala Hare* :// (d F C d)
thebless4ever: Groovy Echo: / istok.de/5804

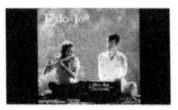

Narayani Ma

-/: *Narayani Narayani Narayani* Ma :/: *Narayani Narayani Narayani Ma* :/ C aC, C e a C
/: *Jay* Ma Jagdambe Jay Ma Jagdambe, *Shakti* Ma Namo *Namah* :/ d, G C
-/: *Narayani Narayani Saraswathi* Ma :/: *Narayani Narayani Saraswathi Ma* :/ C aC, C e a C
/: *Jay* Ma Jagdambe Jay Ma Jagdambe, *Vali* Ma Namo *Namah* :/ d, G C
-/:*Narayani Narayani Mahalakshmi* Ma:/:*Narayani Narayani Mahalakshmi Ma*:/CaC,CeaC
/: *Jay* Ma Jagdambe Jay Ma Jagdambe :/: *Lakshmi* Ma Namo *Namah* :/ d, G C
-/: *Narayani Narayani Durgadevi* Ma :/: *Narayani Narayani Durgadevi Ma* :/ CaC,C e a C
/: *Jay* Ma Jagdambe Jay Ma Jagdambe :/: *Kali* Ma Namo *Namah* :/ d, G C
/: Narayani ...Narayani ...Narayani ...Namo Namah... :/ d F G C
Edo & Jo (Groovy, Echo): / istok.de/6672

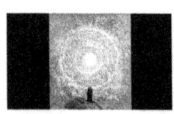

Now I Walk In Beauty

Now I *walk* in *Beauty, Beauty is before* me (d G a, F G a)
Beauty is behind me, *Above and below* me (d G a, F G a)
Libana (Navajo Prayer) (Canon) :d G a, F G a / istok.de/6522-1

Jane Valencia: / istok.de/6522-2

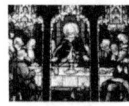

O Christe Domine Jesu

//: O *Christe* Domine *Jesu*,O *Christe* Domine *Jesu* :// (C F, C G)
Taize: C F, C G / istok.de/5930

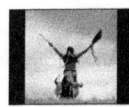

O Great Spirit

O Great Spirit, Earth Sun Sky And *Sea* / a, eGa
You Are Inside, And *All Around Me* / a, eGa
Robert Gass: Also: Dm A / Dm F A / Dm / F Am Dm / istok.de/7300

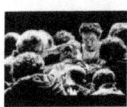

O Lord Hear My Prayer

O *Lord* Hear My Prayer, O *Lord* Hear My Prayer / (a)(d/G)
When I call *answer* me / (C E)
O *Lord* Hear My Prayer, O *Lord* Hear My Prayer / (a)(d/G)
Come and *listen* to *me* / (C E a)
Taize: / istok.de/7135

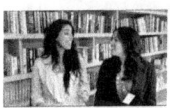

Od Yavo Shalom Alayno

/:*Od* Yavo Shalom Alayno, *Od* Yavo Shalom Alayno (/Aleinu)/C, F
Od Yavo Shalom Alayno, *Ve Alculam* :// C, F GC
//: Salaam Aleno Ve Al Ko Aolam, *Salaam Salaam* :// C F, C F
Lisa Litman: Peace will come to us and all over the
world / istok.de/7319-1

Sheva (Groovy): istok.de/7319-2

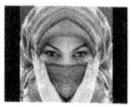

Oh Mata Haidhakandeshvari

Acapella Intro: //: Aya karu Mata...Amba kripa karun janani ://
/: Kalja naru kini Kali Kapanini:/:Karuna maji
Heidakhandeshwari:/
//: *O* Mata *O* Mata Mata, (Sri) *Heidakhandeshwari* :// *(a G)(CEa)*
//: *O* Mata *O* Mata Mata, (Sri) *Heidakhandeshwari* :// *(a G)(CEa)*
Nina Hagen, Moti Maa (Echo, Canon possible too): a G,
CEa / istok.de/5687

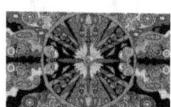

Oh My Celestial Heart

1)*Oh* My *Celestial Heart*, With Your *Love* That *Takes* Me So *High* /(a G a)(C d a)
You *Teach* Me The Way I Can *Live*,You *Show* Me What It *Means* To *Die* /(G e)(F G a)
2)*Oh* my *celestial love*, With your *light* you *heal* my *pain* / (a G a)(C d a)
In your *kingdom* I feel I am *home*, And I *don't* want to *leave* you *again* /(G e)(F G a)
3)*Oh* my *celestial dream*, With your *light* that *shows* me the *way* / (a G a)(C d a)
To *lead* me back home to the *love*, That's *deeper* than *my* words can *say* / (G e)(F G a)
4)*Oh* my *celestial* queen, With your *love* that *takes* me so *high* / (a G a)(C d a)
//: My *heart* has *opened* its *wings*, With *you* I have *learned* how to *fly* ://(G e)(F G a)
Juliana in Peru Pisaq (1/3):(e D e)(G a e),(D h)(C D e)/ istok.de/6736-1

Kundalini Express (1/3): a / C F C / G d C / G a / istok.de/6736-2

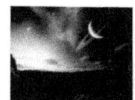

Om Bhagavan

//: *Om* Baghavan, *Sri* Bhaga*van* :// (G d , a G)
//: *Ananda* Baghavan (a G) Satchit*ananda* Bhaga*van* :// (d G)
Maneesh De Moor: / istok.de/7435

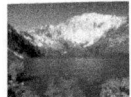

Om Dum Durgayei Namah

//: *Om* Dum Durgayei Namaha (a)
Om Dum Durga*yei* Namaha :// (G a)
Om Dum Durga*yei* Namaha (F G)
Om Dum Durga*yei* Namaha (e a)
Om Dum Durgayei Namaha (A# D#)
Om Dum Durga*yei* - Nama*ha* (G# Fm-C)
+Em D Em/C D Bm Em/F A# D# Cm-G / Dm C Dm/A# C Am Dm/D# G# C# A#m-F
Durga Mantra: / istok.de/5732

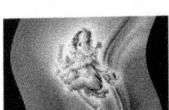

Om Gam Ganapataye Namaha

[//: *Om* Gam Ganapataye Namaha, *Om* Gam Ganapataye Namaha (h, D)
Om Gam Ganapataye Namaha,*Om* Gam Ganapataye Namaha://] x2 (A, h)
[//: *Ganesha Sharanam*, *Ganesha Sharanam* ://] x2 (h D, A h)
Edo & Jo(Echo, Groovy): h D A h / istok.de/6676-1

[//: *Om* Gam Ganapataye Namah, *Om* Sharavanabhavaya Namah (D A)
Om Aim Saraswatyai Namah, *Om* Gum Gurubhyo Namah ://] x3 (e G)
Ganesha, Ganesha....Ganesha, Sharanam Sharanam

Kai and Jasmin (Echo, Groovy): D A e G / istok.de/6676-2

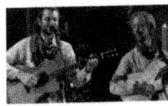

Om Hrim Sum Suryaya Namaha

//: *Om* Hrim *Sum Suryaya Namaha* :// 4x / C a F G
+ "Om Hrim Sum..." rhytmic 4 times per 1 main line
+ *Alleluja, Alleluja, Alleluja, Alleluja* (Instead of "Om Hrim Sum...")
JayJayJay: (Sun Mantra): C a F G / istok.de/6666

57

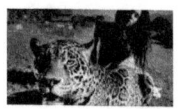

Om Kumara

Om *Kumara* Kushalo Dayayei Namaha (a)
Om *Kumara* Kushalo Dayayei Namaha (e)
Om *Kumara* Kushalo Dayayei Namaha ,(F)
Om *Kumara* Kushalo Dayayei Namaha (e)
Deva Premal & Miten, Maneesh de Moor: / istok.de/7489

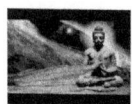

Om Mani Padme Hum

Om Mani Padme Hum (G) *Om* Mani Padme Hum (C)
Om Mani Padme Hum (a) /*Om Mani Padme Mani Padme Hum(Wellness Dreams)*
Om Mani *Padme* Hum (G a)
Jewel in the lotus / Also: (C)(F)(Dm)(C Dm) or (D)(G)(Em)(D
Em): istok.de/7103-1

Nhe Nhang (female voice): / istok.de/7103-2

Deva Premal: a G e a , F e G a / istok.de/7103-3

Wellness Dreams Orchestra:daCG, CGd / istok.de/7103-4

Boris Gebenshikov: A D-A,A E-A / istok.de/7103-5

Kuan Yin Version: a , F e , a d , F e a / istok.de/7103-6

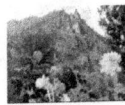

Om Mata Kali Om Mata Durga

Om mata *Kali Om* Mata *Durga, Sara-svati* Te *Namo* Namah/ aFGa, CGCE
Om Mata *Kali Om* Mata *Durga, Para-vati* Te *Namo Namah*/ aFGa, CGCE
Om Bhur Bhuwa Swaha, Tat Savitur Varenyam (a)
Bhargo Devasaya, Dheemahi Dhiyo Yo Naha Prachodayat (a)
Bhakti Music: a F G a, C G C E / istok.de/5859

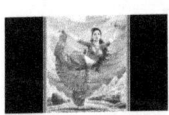

Om Mata Om Kali

//: Om *Mata* Om Kali, *Durga Devi* Na*mo* Nama*ha* :// (e, D H7 e)
Shakti Kunda*lini, Jagadumbe* Ma*ta* (e D, C H7)
He *Shakti* Kunda*lini, Jagadumbe* Ma*ta* (e D, C e)
(+ Tina Malia) //: *Hey* Ma *Durga, Hey* Ma Dur*gaya* :// 4x (e D e)
Jaya Jaga*dumbe* Jagadumbe, Jai Jai *Ma* ... (-e , De)
Amy Barnes Nandini (Groovy): / istok.de/5694-1

 Tina Malia (Groovy): / istok.de/5694-2

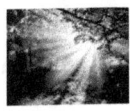

Om Namah Shivaya

Om Namah Shiva , *Om* Namah Shi*vaya* (G)(C D)
Om Namah Shiva , *Shiva Om* Na*mah* (G)(C D G)

59

Robert Gass: C, F G, C, F G C / istok.de/5877

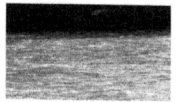

Om Namah Shivaya Shivaya Namah Om

Om Namah *Shivaya, Shivaya* Namah *Om* / aG, dE
Shiva Shiva Shiva *Shivaya, Shivaya Namah* Om / aG, dE
Julia Konon: / istok.de/5882

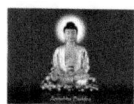

Om Namo Amitabhaya

//: Om Namo *Amitabhaya (a d)*
Buddha Ya *Dharma* Ya *Sangha* Ya :// (a E a)
Om Namo *Om* Namo, *Om* Namo *Amitabhaya* (a G, F E)
Om Namo *Om* Namo (a G)
Om Namo *Amitabhaya* Buddha Ya Dharma Ya Sangha Ya (F E)
Ivan y Tessa: / istok.de/7153-1

Roger Kuhn: / istok.de/7153-2

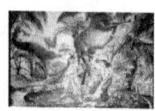

Om Namo Bhagavate Vasudevaya

//: Om namo Bhagavate *Vasudevaya* (a F)
Om namo Bhagavate *Vasudevaya* :// (G a)
//: Vasudevaya Vasudevaya Vasudevaya Om :// (a F G a)
Sahil Jagtiani: a F G a: / istok.de/5722-1

60

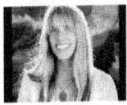

Om Namo Narayanaya

//:*Om Namo Naraya-naya*, *Om Namo Naraya-naya*:// (GCDG,GCDG)
Deva Premal: G C D G / istok.de/5873

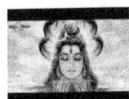

Om Namo Shivaya Gurave

/: *Om* Namo *Shivaya Gurave*, Satchit *Ananda Murtaye* :/ (C G a)(e F)
/:*Namastasye Namastasye Namastasye*, *Namoh Namaha*:/ (C G a)(e F)
Meenakshi C G, a e F / istok.de/5736

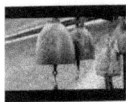

Om Purnam

Om Purnamidah Purnamidam,Purnat Purnamudasyate (aC FE)(aC FE)
Purnasya Purnamidaya,Purnameva - Vashishyate (aC FE)(aC FE)
Satyaa & Pari: a C F E / istok.de/8206

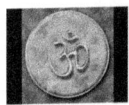

Om Sarve Bhavantu Sukhinah

-*Sarvesham* Svantir Bhavantu (d) *Sarvesham* Shantir Bhavantu (a)
Savresham Purnam *Bhavantu*(FC) *Sarvesham* Mangalam *Bhavantu*/A#d)
-*Sarve* Bhavantu Sukhinah-a (d) *Sarve* Santu Niramayah-a (a)
Sarve Bhadrani *Pasyantu* (FC) *Ma* Kascit Duhkha *Bhaghavet* (A#d)

61

Om *Shanti Shanti Shanti* (dad)
Seven (Echo): / istok.de/8209

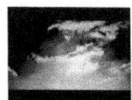

Om Satyam Shivam Sundaram

/: Om *Satyam* Shivam Sundaram,Om *Satyam* Shivam *Sundaram*:/(CGC)
Henry Marshall: C G C G C... / istok.de/5868

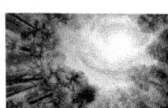

Om Shree Sache Ma

Om shree sache maa Praha*bu* (ad) Ki *jay*(C)
Para *matma* ki *jay* (eF C)
Om shanti shanti shanti, *om* ...(,G-EE7)
Deva Premal: / istok.de/8138

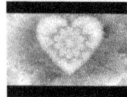

Om Tare Tuttare Ture Soha

Om Tare *Tuttare* (E F#) / (G A) *Ture Soha* (A E) / (C G)
Jaya Laksmi: (E F#)(A E) or (G A) (C G) / istok.de/8119

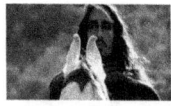

Om Tare Tuttare Ture Svaha

//: Om *Tare* Tut*tare Ture Svaha* (a F G E)
Om *Tare* Tut*tare Ture Svaha* :// (d E F a)
Deva Premal: / istok.de/5682

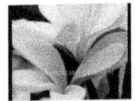

Om Trayambakam

Om Trayambakam *Yajamahe, Sugandim Pushtivardanam* /a D, d aE
Urvarukamiva Bhandanan, *Mrityor* Mukshiya *Mamritate* / a, E a
IndiaJiva: / <u>istok.de/6734-1</u>

Henry Marshall And The Playshop Family: / <u>istok.de/6734-2</u>

Unknown: / <u>istok.de/6734-3</u>

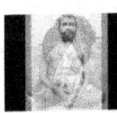

Omkar Guruji

//: Om*kar* Guruji Om*kar* (De) Om*kar* Guru*ji* Om*kar* :// (DAh)
/: Om*kar* Guruji Om*kar* Omkar(Gh) Om*kar* Guruji Om*kar*:/(Gh)
Turkantam: / <u>istok.de/7546-1</u>

Nina Hagen: / <u>istok.de/7546-2</u>

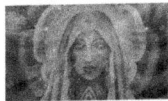

Ong Namo

1)The rain is falling down, Like all the souls you sent here (C)
Coming to this earth, To find healing
Mother earth takes in the rain, Like your heart takes my voice
Let us free eachother, With our prayers, with our voice (...C)

//: And I'm coming home (F) And I'm coming home (C) ://
-//: *Ong* na*mo, guru* **dev** na**mo** :// **(C a, F C) 8x**
-/: **Guru***dev* **Gurudev na***mo* **(C F) Guru***dev* **Gurudev na***mo* :/**(C G)**
2)I bow my head to God. And God took all of me (C a)
Every imperfection. God took all of me (F C)
And every day, God lives and breathes through me (C a)
Looking in the mirror, I love you sweet God (F C)
3)Oh my beloved, Kindness of the heart, I bow to you (C a)
Divine Teacher, Beloved Friend, I bow to you, (I bow to you) (F C) Again and again (C)
Lotus sitting on the water (C F) Beyound time and space (C G)
/: This is your way :/(C F C) /: Ong namo guru dev namo :/ (C a F C)
Snatam Kaur: Only Refrain is also enough ;) / istok.de/8148

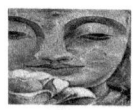

Ong Namo Guru Dev Namo

Ong Namo Guru Dev *Namo,*Ong *Namo* Guru Dev *Namo* /a G a, G a
Ong *Namo* Guru Dev *Namo*, Ong *Namo* Guru Dev *Namo* / G a, G a
Amrit Kirtan (Echo): a G a / istok.de/5792-1

 Mirabei Ceiba (Groovy): d C A# C / istok.de/5792-2
Ong Namo, Guru *Dev* Namo . Guru *Dev* Namo, Guru*deva* (d C).(A# C)

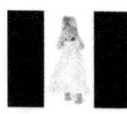

Open my eyes that I may see

Open my eyes, that *I* may see *Glimpses* of truth thou *hast* for me (G D7 D7 G)
Place in my *hands* the *wonderful key* (B7 Em B7 Em)
That shall *unclasp,* and *set* me *free* (A7 D A7 D7)
...*Silently* now I *wait* for thee, *Ready*, my God, thy *will* to see (G D7 D7 G)
...*Open* my eyes, *illumine* me, *Spirit divine* (G7 C D7 G)
Open my ears, that I may hear. Voices of truth Thou sendest clear;
And while the wave notes fall on my ear, Everything false will disappear...*Sile...*
Open my mind, that I may read. More of Thy love in word and deed;
What shall I fear while yet Thou dost lead? Only for light from Thee I plead...*Si..*
Open my mouth, and let me bear, Gladly the warm truth everywhere;

Open my heart and let me prepare, Love with Thy children thus to share...*Silentl*..
The Joslin Grove Choral Society (1/3): / <u>istok.de/6203</u>

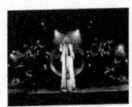

Our Father Who Art In Heaven

Our *Father* who art in *heaven*, *hallowed* be thy Name / C G, C F
Thy *kingdom* come thy will be *done*,on *earth* as in *heaven* (CG, FC)
Give *us* today our daily *bread*, And *forgive* our *sins* / C G, C F
As *we* forgive each *one* of those, who *sins* against *us* (C G, F C)
And *lead* us not to the *tend* of trial,but *deliver* us from *evil* /CG, C F
For *thine* is the *kingdom*, the *power*, and the *glory* (C G, F C)
Cliff Richard (Groovy): C G C F , C G F C / <u>istok.de/5814</u>

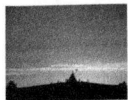

Pacha Mama I'm coming home

/: Pacha *Mama*,I'm coming *home*,To the *place* where I *belong* :/ dCGd
1)I want to be *free*, so *free* Like the *dolphin* in the *sea* / d C G d
Like the *flowers* and the *bees* Like the *birds* in the *trees* / d C G d
I want to fly *high*, so *high* Like an *eagle* in the *sky* / d C G d
and *when* my time has *come* I'm gonna *lay* down and *die* / d C G d
and *when* my time has *come* I'm gonna *rise* up and *fly* /d C G d...Pacha
2)I want to be *free*, be *Me* the *being* that I *see* / d C G d
Not to *rise* and not to *fall* Being *one* and *loving* all / d C G d
There's no *high* There's no *low*, There is no *place* I should *go* /d C G d
/: Just inside a little *star*, Telling me, be *as* you *are* :/ d C G d ...Pacha
Yopi: d C G d / <u>istok.de/6633</u>

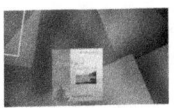

Pavan Pavan Pavan Pavan

Pavan Pavan *Pavan* Pavan *Para* Para *Pavan* Guru (d C d C)
Pavan Guru *Wahe* Guru *Wahe* Guru *Pavan* Guru (d C d C)

Pavan Pavan *Pavan* Pavan *Para* Para *Pavan* Guru (F C d C)
Pavan Guru *Wahe* Guru *Wahe* Guru *Pavan* Guru (F C d C)
Guru Shabad Singh: / istok.de/6714

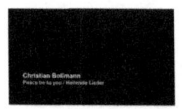

Peace Be To You

1. //: *Light* of heaven *shine* through me (dG)
Lighting up the *world* I *see* (Cad)
And *shine* throughout the *universe* :// (Ea-A7)

2)//: Peace be to *You* Peace be to *me* (dGCa)
Peace be to *all* And the world be *free* :// (Ea-A7)

3)//:*Peace* be *onto You(dGCa)*
Peace be *onto All* I *see*:// (dEa-A7)

4. //: *Living* in the *spirit* of Love, *living* in the *Peace* (dGCa)
Living in the *spirit* of *Happiness* :// (dEa - A7)
Christian Bollman (4 Voices Canon): dGCa dEa-A7 / istok.de/5677-1

Voices of the Heart: / istok.de/5677-2

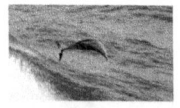

Pritham Bhagautee

Pritham Bhagautee simar kay Guru Naanak Lay dhiaaay
Fir Angad Gur tay Amar Das Ramdas-ay hoay sahai
Arjun Hargobind No simaro Siri Har Rai
Siri Har Krishan Dhiaaee-ai jis dithay sabh dukh jaa-ay
Tegh Bahadur Simaree-ai ghar nau nidh aavay dhaay

66

Sabh thaaee hoay sahaai
Siri Guru Gobind Singh sahib jee sabh thaaee ho-ay sahai
//: Dhan Dhan Siri Guru Grath Sahib Jee :// 4x
Snatam Kaur: a F C G , d F C G/ istok.de/6550 complicate, just Refrain?

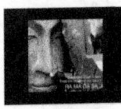

Ra Ma Da Sa Sa Say So Hung

//: *Ra* Ma *Da* Sa *Sa* Say *So* Hung :// (a d E a)
//: *Ra* Ma *Da* Sa *Sa* Say *So* Hung :// (d a C G)
Paramjeet Singh: Ra sun Ma Moon Da earth Sa Infinity: / istok.de/6583-1

 Snatam Kaur: C e F(G)C / F a G F / istok.de/6583-2

 Ajeet Kaur:Eg#c#E,(c#)Ag#c# / GbmEmG,CBmEm/istok.de/6583-3

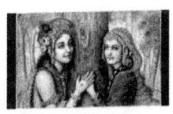

Radhe Radhe Radhe Govinda

//: *Rhade Rhade*, Rhade Govinda :// (d C, G a)
//: *Rhade Rhade*, Rhade Govinda :// (d C, G a)
//: *Rhade Rhade*, Rhade Gopal :// (C G, d F)
Deva Premal: / istok.de/5702

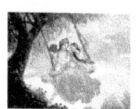

Radhe Radhe Radhe Shyam

Radhe Radhe Radhe Rhade Shyam (x4) / d C A# g A
Govinda Gopala Radhe Radhe Shyam (x4) / A# g C A# A
Govinda Radhe *Radhe* Shyam, *Gopala* Radhe *Radhe* Shyam (4x) / d A#, C d
Vikram Hazra(Groovy): / <u>istok.de/6700-1</u>

Krishna Dhun: f# D, E f# / <u>istok.de/6700-2</u>
/:*Radhe* Radhe Radhe Shyam *Govinda* Radhe Jay Shri *Radhe*, Jay Shri *Radhe:*/
/:*Govinda* Radhe Radhe Shyam *Gopala* Radhe Radhe, Jay Shri *Radhe*, Jay Shri *Radhe:*/

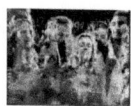

Rainbow Around the Moon

//: *Theres* a *Rainbow*, around the *Moon* :// da, d
Theres a Rainbow, *Theres* a *Rainbow* / da, CG
Theres a *Rainbow*, around the *Moon* / da, d
Rainbow Spirit Oregon: / <u>istok.de/6236</u>

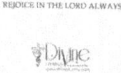

Rejoice in the Lord Always

/: *Rejoice* in the Lord always,And *again* we *sing rejoice:*/ D, G A D
//: *Rejoice* rejoice, and *again* We sing *rejoice* :// D, G A D
Divine Hymns (Groovy Canon): (D-,G A D) / <u>istok.de/6162</u>

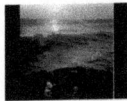

Return Again

//: *Return again, Return again (a E, a E)*
Return to the *land* of your *soul* :// (a E a)
Return to *who* you are, *Return* to *what* you are (a d, a d)
Return to *where* you are, *Born* and re*born* again (a d, a E)
Lyrics byReb Shlomo Carlebach: / istok.de/6258

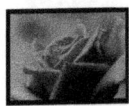

Sa Re Sa Sa

Sa Re Sa Sa,*Sa* Re Sa Sa / *Sa* Re Sa Sa, *Sa* Rung / (G e)(h D)
Har Re Re Har Re Har Re, Har Re Re Har Re Har Re - (C)
Har Re Re Har Re Har Re, *Har* Rung - (G D)
Guru Shabad Singh Khalsa(Groovy): / istok.de/6691-1

 Nirinjan Kaur: C G C G C... / istok.de/6691-2

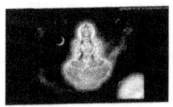

Sarasvati

Sarasvati, Maha Lakshmi, Durga Devi Namaha (a)
Sarasvati Maha *Lakshmi,* Durga *Devi Na-maha* (d a, F Ea)
Henry Marshall And The Playstop Family: / istok.de/5704-1

 Bittu Mallick: / istok.de/5704-2

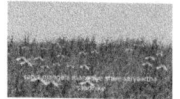

Sarva Mangala Mangalye

Sarva Mangala,Mangalaye ; *Shive,*Sar*vartha* Sadhi*ke* /a, d ; CG, E a
Sharanye Try*ambke, Gauri* / a d , CG
//: *Narayani Namostute* :// / ad , Ea (4x only Tina)
/:*Om* Namah Shivaya (+Tina, Echo),*Om Namah Shivaya*:/4x a,CG
a
Tina Malia (Groovy, Echo): / istok.de/7374-1

Shankari: C a G e / istok.de/7374-2

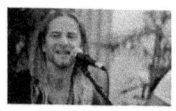

Satchitananda Guru Satchitananda

Satchitananda Guru *Satchitananda (a G)*
Satchitananda Guru *Satchitananda* (a)
//:*Ananda* Guru *Om Shivananda* Guru *Om (*aFGa)
Ananda Guru *Om Shivananda* Guru *Om*:// (FGa)
Kirtan Band (Groovy): / istok.de/6694

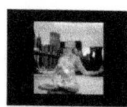

Satyam Shivam Sundaram

/:*Satyam* Shivam *Sundaram, Satyam Shivam Sundaram*:/(a E, F E a)
Satyamayam Shivamayam, Sundaramayam (a E, F E a)
Gyanamayam Premamayam Sarvam Snehamayam (a E, F E a)
/:*Satyam* Shivam *Sundaram, Satyam Shivam Sundaram*:/(a E, F E a)
Guru Charanam *Bhaktimayam, Brahmagyana Mayam* (a E, F E a)
Gurusanidyam Sarvasamatvam, Atmagyanamayam (a E, F E a)
Kundalini Mantra Groovy: (God is Truth is Beauty): a E, F E a / istok.de/5759

70

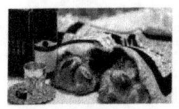

Shalom Aleichem Malachei

1)*Shalom* Alaicheim *Mal'achei* Hasharet,*Mal'achai elyon*/eB7,C B7
Mimelech Mal'chei ham'lachim, hakadosh baruch *hu* / e B7a, C B7
Bo'achem L'shalom *Mal'achei* Hashalom,*Mal'achai elyon*/GD,C B7
Mimelech Mal'chei *ham'lachim, hakadosh baruch hu* / a e, C B7 e
2)Barchuni l'shalom *Mal'achei* Hashalom,*Mal'achai elyon*/eB7,C B7
Mimelech Mal'chei ham'lachim, hakadosh baruch *hu* / e B7a, C B7
Tzeitchem l'shalom *Mal'achei* Hashalom,*Mal'achai elyon*/GD, C B7
Mimelech Mal'chei *ham'lachim, hakadosh baruch hu* / a e, C B7 e
Shalom Aleichem: / istok.de/6669-1

Susana Allen: DA/A-C/d A# C/A# G A/A#Agd / istok.de/6669-2

Peace be upon you (Groovy): / istok.de/6669-3

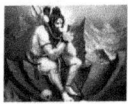

Shiva Maheshwara

Intro: *Shiva* Shankarai Shambo Shambawai Parameshwarai Nama Om (a)
Shiva *Maheshwara* Shiva Maheshwara Shiva Maheshwara *Gurudev* / (aC)
Shiva *Maheshwara* Shiva Shankara Shiva *Mahadeva Gurudev* / (GaGa)
//: *Kailasha* Vasa Mahadeva, Shri *Haidyakhandi* Vasa Sada *Shiva* :// (a)(Ga)
//: Om Tribuvana Pati Samba Sada Shiva :// (a)
//: Shiva *Om* Shiva *Om* Shiva *Om* Shiva *Om*, Baba *Om 4x* Bolla *Om 4x* Namah *Om 4x* ://
/: *Namah* Shivaya *Om Namaha* Shivay Om,*Namaha* Shivaya Om Namah *Om*:/1aC,2GaGa
Goma (Gopal Hari & Ambika)(Groovy): Refr: (CGFa) or (dCFd) istok.de/6537

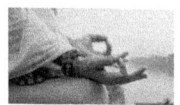

Shiva Shambho

Shiva Shiva Shiva *Shambho*,Shiva* Shiva Shiva *Shambho*/d C,a d
Mahadeva Shambho, Mahadeva Shambo / d C, d *Jaya Jaya Shiva..
Satyaa & Pari (usually Groovy) also e D, H7 e ; e D e: / istok.de/5712

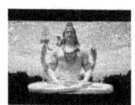

Shiva Shiva Shambho Shankara

Shiva Shiva Shambo Shankara, *Hara* Hara Hara Maha*devaha* / a, E a
Ganga chata dhara *Gouri* Manohara, *Pati* Puri *Parameshwara* / a d, F Ea
Groovy: / istok.de/5710

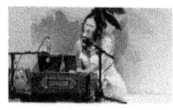

Shivaya Parameshwaraya

Shivaya Parameshwaraya, Chandra*shekharaya* Namah *Om* / a, d a
Bhavaya Bhavaya, Guna *Sambhavaya* / d, a
Shiva *Tandavaya* Namah *Om*,Shiva *Tandavaya* Namah *Om*/d a,d a
Satyadevi: / istok.de/6488-1

Vani Devi & Narayan (Echo): / istok.de/6488-2

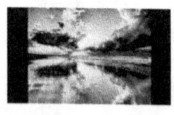

Shivoham

Sachara chara para *purna,Shivoham*, Shivoham(a G, F -E- a)
Nityananda Swarupa...Shivoham, Shivoham (a G, F -E- a)

//: *Anandoham Anandoham* :// (1 a G / 2 F E a)2x
//: *Shivoham, Shivoham* :// (1 a G, 2 F E a)2x
Snatam Kaur & Manish Vyas (Groovy): a G / F E a / <u>istok.de/7095</u>

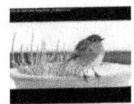

Shri Guru Sharanam

Shri Guru Sharanam, *Namo* Namo Namah / a, d
Shri Guru Sharanam, *Namo* Namo Namah / G, E
+: Sat Guru,Atma Guru,Ishta Guru,Shri Shri Guru,Jagat Guru
Christina Schwalbach: / <u>istok.de/6502</u>

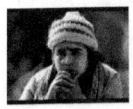

Shri Guru Sharanam Mangalam

Shri *Guru* Sharanam, *Sadguru Sharanam* / a d, e a
Guru Om Guru *Om*, *Guru* Om *Mangalam* / a d, e a
Emam & Friends: a d, e a / <u>istok.de/6493-1</u>

Moti Maa (Groovy): a F E a, a G E a / <u>istok.de/6493-2</u>

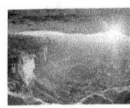

Sing Hallelujah to the Lord

Sing Halle*lujah* to the *Lord* / a E a
Sing Halle*lujah* to the *Lord* / C G E
Sing Halle*lujah Sing* Halle*lujah* / F C d a
Sing Halle*lujah* to the *Lord* / a E a
Also: Jesus is risen from the dead,
Jesus is living in His church, Jesus is coming for His own

...Sing Alleluja unserm Herrn, Poj Alleluja Gospodu, Canta Aleluia al Senhor
With Echo: / istok.de/5714-1

 5 Sisters: / istok.de/5714-2

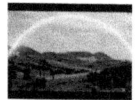

Somewhere Over the Rainbow

1)Somewhere over the rainbow (G D C) Way up high (G)
And the dreams that you dream of (C G) Once in a lullaby... (D Em C)
Oh, somewhere over the rainbow (G D C) Blue birds fly (G)
And the dreams that you dream of (C G) Dreams really do come true... (D Em C)
2)Someday I'll wish upon a star (G) Wake up where the clouds are far behind me (D Em C)
Where trouble melts like lemon drops (G) High above the chimney tops (D)
That's where you'll find me (Em C) Oh, somewhere over ...
3)Someday I'll wish upon a star (G) Wake up where the clouds are far behind me (D Em C)
Where trouble melts like lemon drops (G) High above the chimney tops (D)
That's where you'll find me (Em C) Oh, somewhere over ...
Israel Kamakawiwo'Ole: / istok.de/6126

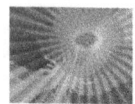

Song For The Sun

Sun in the Sky, *hangs* on our *cross* / A F A
With out its light and love *surely* we are *lost* / A F A
Grows all our food for *everything* we eat / A F A
Keeps us warm and *gives* us its heat / A F A
...And now *this* is a *song* for the *Sun* / D F C G
...*This* is a *song* for *our* one *Sun* / D F C G
The Sun has given freely to all men in all times / A F A
Why has man forgot cant he see the signs? / A F A
Has he been mislead or is he blind? / A F A
...But now remember the song for the Sun / D F C G
...Remember the song for our one Sun / D F C G

74

Leave the darkness, become one with the light / A F A
You don't need the book to tell you its right / A F A
Why is there no day given to the sun? / A F A
Why is there no thanks given to our one? / A F A
...And now celebrate the Sun on Sunday / D F C G
...Give thanks for the Sun on Sunday / D F C G
...Sing the song for the Sun / D F C G
SunGypsy: istok.de/6553

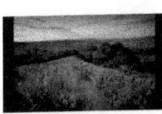

Song of Shiva

Chidananda roopah *shivoham shivoham,Chidananda* roopah *shivoham shivoham*(CFG),(CFC)
1) Manobuddhi ahamkara chita ni naham, Nachashotre jiv-hey nachaghrana netre
Nacha vioma bhoomir na tejoe na vayu. Chidananda roopah shivoham shivoham
2) Nachaprana saugno na va puncha vayu, Navah sapto dhatoo navaa puncha koshah
Na waak pani paadam nachapasta paayu. Chidananda...
3) Na me dvasha rago na me lobha mo-hoe, Mado naiva me naiva matsarya bhava
Na dharmo na chartoe na kaarno na Moksha. Chidananda...
4) Na punyam na paapam na saukyum na dhukham,Na mantro na tirtham name daa na yug na ha
Aham bhoja namnaiva bhojyam na bhokta. Chidananda...
5) Na mrootyur na shanka na me jaati bheda, Pita naiva me naiva maata na janma
Na bandhur na mitram gurunaiva shishya. Chidananda...
6) Aham nirvekalpo nirakaara roopo, Vibureviapya sarvatra sarvendriyani
Sadame samatvah na muktir na bandha. Chidananda...
Deva Premal: each line: (C F G) , (C, F C) / istok.de/8194

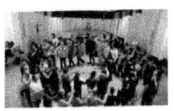

Spirallied von Iria

Ich *gehe* und *gehe*, *weite* die *Kreise*, *gehe* zum *Ursprung* und *Ziel* / a E, a E, a G C
Ich *gehe* die *Pfade*, der *grossen Spirale*, und *singe* das *uralte Lied* / d G, C a, d E a
Iria: / istok.de/5836

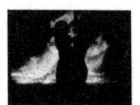

Spirits of fire come to us

/:Spirits of fire come to us,We will kindle the fire:/(Bm D Bm)(A (F#) Bm)
We will kindle the fire, Dance the magic circle around (Em Bm)(A Bm)
We will kindle the fire, We will kindle the fire (Em Bm)(A (F#) Bm)
Trigoddess (Canon)(Female Voices): / istok.de/6362-1

Anam Cara (Male Voices): / istok.de/6362-2

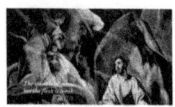

Stay With Me

Stay with *me*, *Remain* here with *me* / a E, a E
Watch and pray, *Watch* and *pray* / aG CE, aG E7
Bleibet hier, und *wachet* mit *mir, Wachet* und *betet, Wachet* und *betet*
Nie boj sie, *nie* lekaj sie, *Bog* sam *wystarczy, Bog* sam *wystarczy(PL)*
Taize: / istok.de/6289

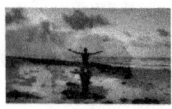

Swami we adore You

*Swami** (I), We *adore You* (Cd, G C)
Lay (my) our *live*(s), *before You* (C d, G C)
How we (I), *love You* (C d, G C)   *...Father...Jesus,...Spirit...
Canon: C d G C / istok.de/5716

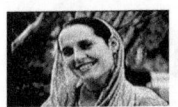

Sweet Chant (Hare Krishna)

Hare Krishna Hare Krishna(a) Krishna Krishna(a) Hare Hare(a)
Hare Rama Hare Rama (d) *Rama* Rama (d) *Hare* Hare (E)
Vraja, Shashika Mooruth: a - d E / <u>istok.de/5794</u>

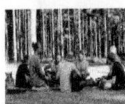

Tall Tree Warm Fire

Tall *trees* deep *water*, Strong *wind* warm *fire* / a e, a e
I *feel* it in my *body*, I *feel* it in my *soul* / C G, F a
Heya heya heya heya. Heya heya ho / a
Heya heya heya heya *ho* / Ga
Rainbows (Groovy): / <u>istok.de/6441-1</u>

Gila Antara (Groovy): a e, a e, C G, F a / a, G a / <u>istok.de/6441-2</u>

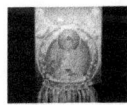

Teyata Om Bekanze

Teyata Om Bekanze, Bekanze, Maha Bekanze / d
Radza Samudgate *Soha* / a
Deva Premal (Groovy): d......a / <u>istok.de/5843</u>

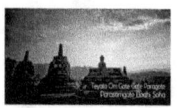

Teyata Om Gate Gate

Teyata Om Gate Gate, *Paragate Parasamgate, Bodhi* Soha / G, D e, C
Teyata Om *Gate* Gate, Paragate *Parasamgate, Bodhi Soha* / G e, G CG, a G
Praja Paramita (1/3): / istok.de/6128

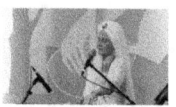

The Angels are Listening

The Angels are *Listening* (C) God is *listening* (e)
I am *listening* (C) *Sun*-ai... (e C E C e...)
Suniai sidh peer sur naath (C) *Suniai* dharat dhaval aakaas (e)
Suniai deep loa paataal (C) *Suniai* pohe na sakay kaal (e)
Naanak bhagtaa sadaa vigaas (F) *Suniai* dookh paap ka naas (G)
Naanak bhagtaa sadaa vigaas (C) *Suniai* dookh paap ka naas (e)
Naanak bhagtaa sadaa vigaas (F) *Suniai* dookh paap ka naas (G)
Suni-ai... (e C E C e...)
All my pain departs (C) in *listening* to my heart (e)
Sanatam Kaur: / istok.de/6306-1

Snatam Kaur Suni-Ai Celebration: / istok.de/6306-2

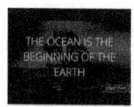

The Ocean is the Beginning of the Earth

//: The *Ocean* is the *Beginning* of the *Earth* :// a G a
//: *All* Life *Comes* From the *Sea* :// F G a
Pagan Chant: / istok.de/6409-1

Jay & Jay (Echo): / <u>istok.de/6409-2</u>

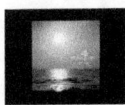

The Ocean refuses no river

//: The *Ocean refuses* no *river*, no *river* :// (C F G, C)
//: The *Open* heart, *refuses* no part of *me*, no *part* of you :// (F, a G,-e- F)...
//: *Guru Guru Wahe Guru*, Guru *Ramdas Guru* :// (C G C G, CG CG)
//: *Guru* Guru *Wahe* Guru, Guru Ramdas *Guru* :// (F a, Ge F)
Mirabai Ceiba: / <u>istok.de/6498</u>

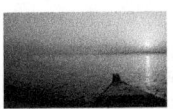

The River is flowing

1)The *river* is flowing, *flowing* and *growing* (a G a)
The *river* is flowing *back* to the *sea* (G a)
Mother earth *carry* me, your *child* I will *always* be (C a G a)
Mother earth carry me *back* to the *sea* (a G a)
2)The *Moon*, she is waiting, *waxing* and *waning* (a G a)
The *Moon*, she is waiting, for *us* to be free (G a)
Sister Moon watch *over* me,a *child* I will *always* be (C a G a)
Sister Moon watch over me, *until* we are *free* (a G a)
3)The *Sun*, he is shining, *brightly* he's *shining* (a G a)
The Sun, he is shining, lightning the way (G a)
Father Sun,shine over me,your child I will always be(Ca G a)
Father Sun, shine over me, until we can see! (a G a)
4)The Fire is burning, destroying and healing (a G a)
The Fire is burning, for us to be pure (G a)
Violet Flame burn over me, a child I will always be (C a G a)
Violet Flame burn over me, until we are pure (a G a)

5)Das Wasser,dass will fliessen,Fliessen,sich ergiessen(aGa)
Das Wasser, dass will fliessen. Zurück in das Meer (G a)
Mutter Erde führe mich.Dein Kind werd Ich immer sein (CaGa)
Mutter Erde führe mich. Zurück in das Meer (a G a)
Sangeeta: / istok.de/5706-1

Wake Up songs: / istok.de/5706-2

Line Halstad & Hallgeir Bjerke: / istok.de/5706-3

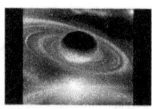

The Universe Is Singing

//: The *universe* is singing a *song* (D G) The *universe* is dancing *along* (A D)
The *universe* is *singing* on a *day* like *this* (loughing) :// (h G A D)
And its *high time* to *dance*/ x3(sing, lough) (DGA) So *wake* up and *dance* (GA)
Peter Makena (Groovy): / istok.de/7837-1

Dr. Roland Schutzbach: / istok.de/7837-2

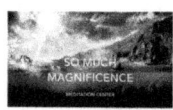

There is So Much Magnificence

There is *So Much Magnificence*,In the Ocean(D A h f#,G-D)
Waves Are Coming In, *Waves* Are Coming In (e A)
//: *Hallelujah, Hallelujah* :// (D A b f#, G e G A)
Deva Premal & Miten: D A b f# G D e A / istok.de/6445-1

80

Shimon Lev Tahor (Canon): / istok.de/6445-2

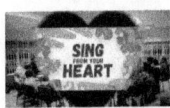

There's a Jewel In The Lotus Flower Unfolding

Hari *Om* Mani Om Mani Padme Om Om Mani,*Om* Mani Padme *Om* (d, C d)
There's a *Jewel* In The Lotus Flower Unfolding, *Deep* Within My *Soul**
To Be a *Jewel* In The Lotus Flower *Unfolding*, Is The *Highest* Goal...Hari..
London heart Group(Groovy): d C or (a G)*Deep in my
Heart/ istok.de/6411-1

 Bodywisdom School(Groovy): / istok.de/6411-2

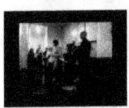

Thy light is in all forms

//: Thy *light* in all forms (a) Thy *love* in all *beings* :// (d E)
//: *Hu* Allah Hu Allah *Hu* Allah Hu :// (a E a)
//: Dein *Licht* ist in allen Formen (a)
Deine *Liebe* in allen Wesen (d E)...Hu Allah...(a E a)
Kiria & Stefan Live Workshop: / istok.de/8171-1

 Hazrat Inayat Khan,Barbara Reischl,Rudolf Zauner: / istok.de/8171-2

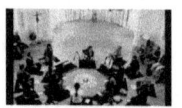

Tief in mir

Tief in mir *bin* ich Kraft, *bin* ich Liebe *vom* Licht bewacht /a d G E-E7
(Tief in dir bist du...Tief in uns....sind wir...)
Ja wir öffnen unsere *Herzen, feiern* unser wahres *Sein* / a d G E - E7
Liebe wohnt in allen *Wesen, und* in ihr sind wir *daheim* / a d G E - E7
Iria: a d G E - E7 / istok.de/5834

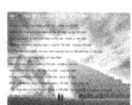

To the One

We are on this *journey home* to the *one* - home to the *one*
Looking here and *searching* there *all* for the *one* - all for the *one*
Many lives spent *on* this road *home* to the *one* - home to the *one*
Nightless nights and *dayless* days in *love* for the *one* - love for the *one*
Let this heart find *peace* and *rest* in the *one* - here in the *one*
-Shri Ram, *Jaya* Ram, *Jaya* Jaya Ram, *Om* jaya *Ram*...
We are on this *journey home* to the *one* - home to the *one*
Who has ever *seen* this love *melt* into *one* - melt into *one*
Bodies come and *bodies* go *all* to the *one* - all to the *one*
While *nothing* ever *really happened here* in the *one* - *here in the one*
I,Me,Mine and *You* and Yourself all *dance* in the *one-d*ance in the one
Dance in the one (simult.: Shri Ram, Jaya Ram, Jaya Jaya Ram...)
We are on this journey home to the one
Looking here and *searching* there *O* For the *one* - For the *one*
Satyaa & Pari: a F C G - a / istok.de/8182

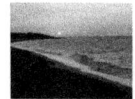

Tui Amoris Ignem

Veni Sancte Spiritus, Tui Amoris Ignem Accende / a F GE, a F G E
Veni Sancte Spiritus, Veni Sancte Spiritus / a F GC, a F Ea
Taize: / istok.de/6292-1

Holy Spirit come to *us*, *Kindle* in *us* the *fire* of your *love*/aFGE, aFGE

Holy Spirit come to *us*, *Holy Spirit come* to *us* / a F G C, a F E a

Taize English: / istok.de/6292-2

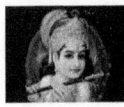

Tum Hi Ho Mata

//: *Tum* Hi Ho *Mata*, *Pita* Tum *Hi* Ho :// (a d, E a)
//: *Tum* Hi Ho *Bandhu*, *Saka* Tum *Hi* Ho :// (a d, E a)
1)Tum hi ho sathi tumhi sahare, Koi na apna siva tumhare
Tum hi ho naiya tum hi khevaiya,Tum hi ho bandhu sakha...
2)Jo kjil sake na vo ful ham hai, Tumhare charno ki dhul ham hai
Daya ki drishti sadahi rakhna, Tum hi ho bandhu sakha tum hi ho
...N*amah* S*hivay* Om, N*amah* S*hivay* Om
Lata Mangeshkar: a d E a: / istok.de/5718-1

Ananda (Modern groovy western version): / istok.de/5718-2

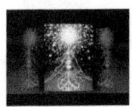

Tumare Darshan

//: Tumare *darshan* ki bela, ye mausam *raas* rachane *ka* :// (A, dA)
//: Liye *ullas* ki sanse, samay *masti* me jine *ka* :// (A, dA)
Deva Premal: / istok.de/5875

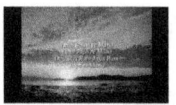

Tumi Bhaja Re Mana

//: Tumhi *Bhajere* Ma Nam Tumhi *Japare* Ma Na / e C
Om *Shri* Ram Jaya Ram *Japare* Ma *Nam* :// h C e
//: Tumhi *Bhajere* Ma Nam Tumhi *Japare* Ma Na / a e
Om *Shri* Ram Jaya Ram *Japare* Ma *Nam* :// h C e
Manish Vyas (Echo): / istok.de/5762

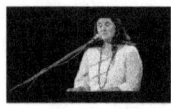

Twameva Mata

Twameva Mata, Cha *Pita Twameva* / C a, d G
Twameva Bandu, Cha *Sakha Twameva* / C a, d C
Twameva Vidya, *Dravinam Twameva* / C a, d G
Twameva Sarvam, Mama *Deva Deva* / C a, d C
Sacred Earth(elody:Ananda Rupam): Also: G h C G / istok.de/7324-1

Sudha & Maneesh De Moor: C a G, G C / istok.de/7324-2

Deva Premal same as Sudha & Manish: / istok.de/7324-3

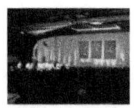

Ubi Caritas

Ubi Caritas, Et *Amor* / C Ga, FCG
Ubi Caritas, *Deus ibi est* / C Ga, F G C
Taize: / istok.de/5720

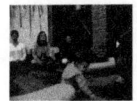

Uma Parvati Ananda Ma

//: *Uma* Parvati, *Ananda Ma* :// C, F C
//: *Kali* Durge, *Namo Namah* :// C, G C
Om Namah Shivaya, *Namah Shivaya* (x2) / C, F C
Om Namah Shivaya, *Namah Shivaya* (x2) / C, G C
Shambhava: / istok.de/6388

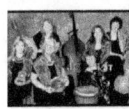

Under the Full Moonlight

Under the full moon light we dance Spirits
Dance we dance, Joining, Hands we Dance, Joining, souls rejoice
Libana: (Canon) e (D) or acapella / istok.de/6547

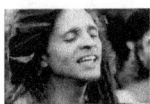

Universal Lover

You Are My Mother You Are My Father / d
You Are My Lover You Are My Friend / C d
In The Beginning You Are The Centre / d
And You Are Beyond The End / C d
And I Love You So 'Cos You Helped Me See / d C d
To See You In All Is To See You In Me / d C d
I'm In You And You're In Me / C d

1)You are the colors of the rainbow. You are the pure white light in me
You are the rivers, you are the mountains, you're the sky, you are the sea
2)And I love you so... You help me see, To see you in all... Is to see you in me
I'm in you and you're in me, I'm in you and you're in me
3)The branches of a tree. They may be many, But the tree, you know my friend, is one.
The petals of a lotus, have you noticed, are many, But the lotus is one
4)Gurus and swamis, teachers are many. But the truth is one
Prophets, religions, Lord, there's so many, But God is one

85

5)And I want to touch you, I want to feel you, I want to be right by your side
I'm want to know you, love you, I'm going to serve you all the time
Rainbow Spirit: / istok.de/6139

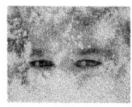

Vibhuti Mantram

Paramam Pavitram Baba Vibhutim / C,
Paramam Vichitram *Lila Vibhutim* / d G C
Paramartha Ishtartha Moksha Pradattam / C
Baba Vibhutim *Idam Ashrayami* / d G C
Sai Baba: / istok.de/5727

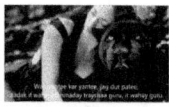

Wah Yantee

Waa yantee kar *yantee*, jag dut *patee*, aadak *it waha* / C G a-e, C G, a G
brahmaday trayshaa *guroo*, *it* wa*hay* gu*roo* / CG d, a e a-G
Aquarian Sadhana: / istok.de/7363-1

Amrit Kirtan: / istok.de/7363-2

1)*Wah yantee* kar *yantee*, jag dut *patee*, *aadak* it *waha* / a G a, G, F C
brahmaday, tray*shaa goroo* , *it* wa*hay, guroo* / da, C G , F a, G
2)*Wah* yantee *kar* yantee, *jag* dut *patee* , *aadak* it *waha* / C G, d FG, C G
brahmaday, tray*shaa goroo* , *it wahay*, gu*roo* / dF, C G , FC, G

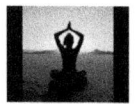

Wahe Guru Wahe Jio

Wahe Guru Wahe Guru, Wahe Guru Wahe Jio x2 / a F a F, a F a F

Wahe Guru Wahe Guru,Wahe Guru Wahe Jio x2 /G F G F, G F G-e
Snatam Kaur: Indescribably Great is The Wisdom 0f My
Soul: / istok.de/6561

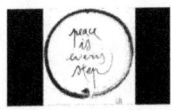

Way of the Heart

Let the *way* of the heart, let the *way* of the heart (e)(D)
Let the *way* of the *heart*, Shine *through* (C D)(e)
Love upon *love* upon *love*, *All* hearts are *beating* as *one* (GDe)(C De)
Light upon *light* upon *light*,*Shining* as *bright* as the *sun*(G D e)(C D e)
Wake Up songs: / istok.de/6181

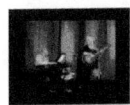

We All Come From God

/: We *all* come from *God*, And *unto* God we *return* :/d a, G a
Like a *stream, flowing* to the *ocean / da, G a*
Like a *ray* of *light*, *returning* to the *sun* / d a, G a
Christina Quinn: d a G a / istok.de/6339

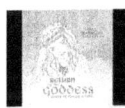

We All Come From The Goddess

We All Come From The Goddess, And To Her We *Shall Return* / d, C d
Like a Drop Of Rain Flowing *To* the *Ocean* / C d
We All Come From The One God, And To Him We *Shall Return* /d,C d
Like a Spark Of Fire Reaching *For* The Open *Sky* / C d
We All Come From One, And To One We *Shall Return* / d, C d
Like a *Ray* Of Light Reaching *For Eternity* / C d
Lindie Lila: / istok.de/6327

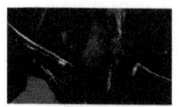

We are as God created us

//: *We* are / (*I* am) as god *created* (us) me (G a)
In the *love* in the light in the *glory* :// (C G)
//: *In* the love in the light in the glory (x3) (1x-G, 2x-a, 3x-C)
We are (*I* am) :// (G)
Jay Jay Jay (Groovy) (Also called: In the Glory) (G a C G): / istok.de/7674

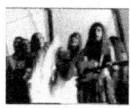

We Are One in Harmony

We Are One in *Harmony* Singing in *Celebration* / D C G D
We Are One in *Harmony Singing* in *Love* / D C G D
Rainbow Spirit Oregon: D C G D / istok.de/6575

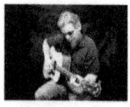

We Are One In The Spirit

1)We are *one* in the Spirit, we are one in the Lord / Em
We are *one* in the Spirit, we are one in the Lord / Am Em
And we *pray* that all unity may one *day* be restored / Am Em
And they'll *know* we are *Christians* by our *love*, by our love / C Em Am
Yes they'll know we are Christians by our *love* / Em Am Em
2)We will all *walk* together We will walk hand in hand / Em
We will all *walk* together We will *walk* hand in hand / Am Em
And *together* we'll share these blessings....*God* is in the land / Am Em
For we *know* we are *God's* children By our *Love*, by our Love / C Em Am
Yes, we *know* we're *God's* children By our *Love* / Em Am Em
3)We will *work* with each other We will work side by side / Em
We will *work* with each other We will *work* side by side / Am Em
And *restore* each one's dignity By *finding* God inside / Am Em
For we *know* we are *God's* children By our *Love*, by our Love / C Em Am
Yes, we *know* we're *God's* children By our *Love* / Em Am Em

Jack Marti: / istok.de/6206

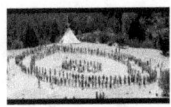

We are opening

//: *He* jonge Ho jonge He jong jong :// (a)
The *earth* is our mother We must take care of her (a)
The *earth* is our mother We must take *care* of *her* (a G a)..He jonge.(2x)..
Her *sacred* ground we walk upon with every step we take (a)
Her *sacred* ground we walk upon with every *step* we *take* (a G a)
We are *opening* up in sweet surrender, to the *luminous* love light *of* the One(aGa)
//: We are opening, we are opening :// (a G a)
Rainbow Family Songs / a / a G a: / istok.de/5646-1

Traditional Native American: / istok.de/5646-2

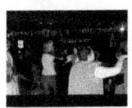

We are the Rising Sun

We are the rising* sun, We are the change / C
We are the ones We've been *waiting* for / C F
And *we* are...Dawning!!! / G // *also "light of the sun"
Words and Music by Raven (Groovy): / istok.de/6296

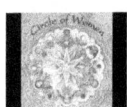

We Shall Lift Each Other Up

Humble Yourself In the *Sight* Of The *Sister*, *Bend* Down Low / a G a, E
Humble Yourself In the *Sight* Of The *Brother*, *You* Got To Know What She Knows / aGa,E
(...Mother-Father, Parents-Children, Mountain-Ocean ...)
We Shall *Lift* Each Other *Up*, *Higher* And Higher / F G a, E
We Shall *Lift* Each Other *Up* / F G a, -E

89

Alice Di Micele (Groovy): (Also known as Humble Yourself) / <u>istok.de/7232-1</u>

Anja Daniel (vocal) Charles Jenks (Groovy): / <u>istok.de/7232-2</u>

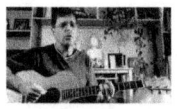

Who Is In My Temple

Who is in my *Temple*, *Who* is in my *Temple* (G e)(G e)
All the doors do *open* themselves (G e)
All the lights do *light themselves* (G D e)
Darkness like a dark bird, *Flies away flies away* (D)(G e G e)
Act on Wisdom (1/3): / <u>istok.de/6209</u>

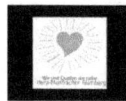

Wir sind Quellen der Liebe

Wir sind Quellen, *Quellen* der Liebe (a d)
Voll *Freude* und *Glückseligkeit* (G C)
So *lasst* unser *Leben* in *Strom* der Liebe *sein* (a d G C)
Dann *fliesst* er so*gleich* in das *Meer* der Liebe *ein* (a d E a)
Liebe, Liebe wachse! Liebe, vermehre dich! (2x) (a G a, a G a)
//: Fliesse ein in das *Meer* der *göttlichen Liebe* (d G C a)
V*erschmelze, werde eins* :// (d, E a)
Herz-Mantrachor Nürnberg: / <u>istok.de/5699</u>

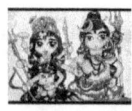

Ya Devi Sarva Bhuteshu

Ya *Devi* Sarva*bhuteshu*, *Shakti Ru*pena S*ansthita* / d C, E a

//: Namastasyayi Namastasyayi Namastasyayi Namo Namaha ://4x dCEa
Ya *Devi* Sarva*bhuteshu, Lakshmi* Rupena *Sansthita...*
Ya *Devi* Sarva*bhuteshu, Shanti* Rupena *Sansthita...*
Tina Malia + Shimshay (Groovy): Namastasye
Namonamaha / istok.de/7371

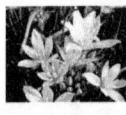

Yemaya Assessu

Yemanhya Asesu, Asesu Yemanhya / G C, D G
Yemanhya Olodo, Olodo Yemanhya / e a, D G
Deva Premal (Prayer and a worship in the Yoruba
religion): / istok.de/6349

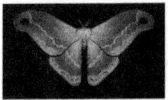

You are forever pure Suddhossi

Buddhossi

//: Sud*dhossi* Bud*dhossi* Niran*j*anos*i* / D a7, De
Sam*sara* ma*ya*, Pari*var* jitos*i* / D a7, D e
Sam*sara* svapa*nam*, Traija *mohan* nid*ram* / D a7, D e
Na *janma* mri*tyor*, Tat *sat* sva ru*pe*://4x / D a7, D e
...You *are* forever *pure*, you *are* forever *true* / D a7, D e
and the *dream* of this *world,* can *never* touch *you* / D a7, D e
So *give* up your *attachments*, *give* up your *confusion* / Da7,De
And *fly* in that *space,* that's *beyond* all *illusion* / D a7, D e
Shimshai: D a7 D e / istok.de/6544-1

  Video lyrics: D a7 D e / istok.de/6544-2

TABLE OF CONTENT: (>> - Echo; ∞ - Canon; ! - Groovy)

92

93

RAINBOWSONGS.ORG

Please register on https://rainbowsongs.org to submit songs with Your Name (or anonymously).

Write me please a message if new songs only, should build a book2 or extend „all in one" 2 edition.

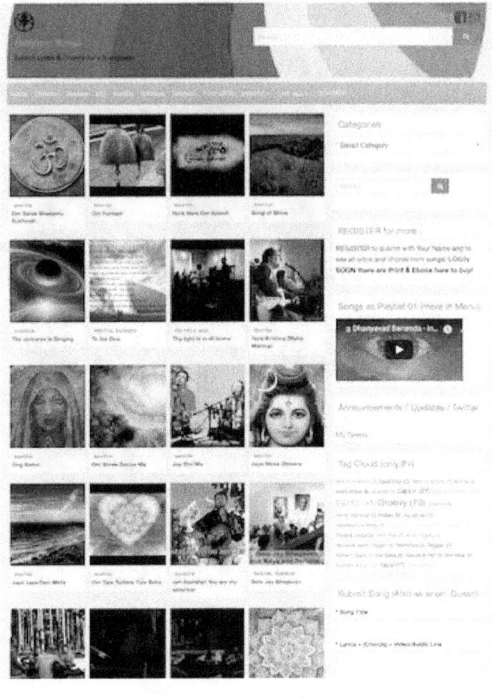

Impr.:Jaroslaw Istok;Martin-Luther-Str.16;10777 Berlin;ananda@rainbowsongs.org+4917649664422